How to Make School Make Sense

of related interest

Create a Reward Plan for Your Child with Asperger Syndrome
John Smith, Jane Donlan and Bob Smith
ISBN 978 1 84310 622 7

**Playing, Laughing and Learning with Children
on the Autism Spectrum**
A Practical Resource of Play Ideas for Parents and Carers
2nd Edition
Julia Moor
ISBN 978 1 84310 608 1

Reaching and Teaching the Child with Autism Spectrum Disorder
Using Learning Preferences and Strengths
Heather MacKenzie
ISBN 978 1 84310 623 4

A Will of His Own
Reflections on Parenting a Child with Autism – Revised Edition
Kelly Harland
Foreword by Jane Asher, President of the National Autistic Society
ISBN 978 1 84310 869 6

Why do I have to?
A Book for Children Who Find Themselves Frustrated by Everyday Rules
Laurie Leventhal-Belfer
Illustrated by Luisa Montaini-Klovdahl
ISBN 978 1 84310 891 7

How to Make School Make Sense

A Parents' Guide to Helping the
Child with Asperger Syndrome

Clare Lawrence

Foreword by Tony Attwood

Jessica Kingsley Publishers
London and Philadelphia

First published in 2008
by Jessica Kingsley Publishers
116 Pentonville Road
London N1 9JB, UK
and
400 Market Street, Suite 400
Philadelphia, PA 19106, USA

www.jkp.com

Library of Congress Cataloging in Publication Data
Lawrence, Clare.
 How to make school make sense : a parents' guide to helping the child with
Asperger syndrome / Clare Lawrence.
   p. cm.
 ISBN 978-1-84310-664-7 (pb : alk. paper) 1. Autistic children--Education.
2. Education--Parent participation. 3. Asperger's syndrome in children. I.
Title.
 LC4717.L39 2008
 371.94--dc22

                                              2008009964

British Library Cataloguing in Publication Data
A CIP catalogue record for this book is available from the British Library

ISBN 978 1 84310 664 7

Printed and bound in the United States by
Thomson-Shore, 7300 Joy Road, Dexter, MI 48130

For Aidan

Acknowledgements

I should like to thank a number of people who have supported the writing of this book, especially Jan Campito for so kindly giving her time and expertise to help me navigate across the various language and cultural pitfalls which I encountered.

Thank you also to all the people who read through the manuscript and gave me such good advice and encouragement.

I wish to thank all the parents, teachers, teaching assistants and children who have been willing to share their problems and solutions with me, and who have been so welcoming to me in the various schools I have visited. You are too many to mention by name, but you are the sources of all the good ideas in this book. Keep up the good work!

Particular thanks for all the inspiration 'on the ground' to Claire Thorley, Jamie Grossmith, Mark Anderson, Clare Camp, Rebecca Mills and Paula Kingman.

Thank you, too, to Sam for his contribution to Chapter 4, and to my family – for everything.

Contents

Foreword

It is rare for a child with Asperger syndrome to enjoy being at school. Almost every morning parents have to reassure the child before they go to primary school that he or she will be able to cope with the lessons, behaviour of the other children and sensory experiences and that the teacher does understand the child's experiences and perspective. At the end of the school day, parents have to cope with an emotionally and physically exhausted child, repair their son or daughter's emotions and explain aspects of the day that have been confusing or frustrating for the child. This is the typical daily routine for parents of a child with Asperger syndrome.

But it does not have to be that way. Clare Lawrence is a parent of a child with Asperger syndrome, and a teacher. She understands the perspectives of parents, teachers, school administrators and children with Asperger syndrome. She has combined this knowledge to write an excellent book on how to make school make sense for such children. The text has many practical suggestions that will significantly improve the quality of life for children, families and teachers. We have had to wait a long time for such a book, and at last it is here.

Professor Tony Attwood

Preface

This book is for parent(s) of a child with Asperger syndrome (AS), who are faced with the problem of how to support that child as he deals with the challenging and often confusing subject of school. A basic level of knowledge about AS is presupposed in the reader. When we first receive the diagnosis of AS in our child it can be a stunning blow. However, from my experience many parents move very quickly from a state of shock to becoming near-experts about AS. I have known parents read every book, attend every workshop and obtain every available qualification about AS. Within 18 months, parents may well be a highly knowledgeable and 'clued-up' group of people.

This book does not, therefore, describe the symptoms or attributes of AS. It does not even list the (many) problems that a child with AS might encounter at school. What it does do is come up with practical, accessible suggestions of ways to make that child's time at school 'make more sense'.

It is aimed at the parents for the simple reason that it is parents who have the greatest motivation to help their child. Parents – and by 'parents' I mean anyone who has parental care of a child – stay the course. It may be very difficult to achieve 'joined-up care' for the child with AS through the various classes, years and stages of his educational life. Until he is able to provide that continuity himself, only the parent is likely to be there to do it for him.

This book also includes parents as the 'other half' of the child's education. What is needed so desperately is consistency for the child with AS across different aspects of his life. The normal inconsistencies between home and school, understood by the neurotypical child, will be an anathema to the child with AS. At its simplest, if the rule taught at school is to put your hand up before asking a question, the child with AS may use that behaviour across all environments unless supported not to. At a more complex level, AS occurs across all social and ethnic boundaries. What if the social culture of home is that it is rude to look directly into an adult's eyes? How confusing is it going to be for the child with AS, educated within a different social culture, to be reprimanded for not meeting the teacher's gaze?

Teachers are just that – teachers. They are not medics. It can be daunting for teachers to feel that they are responsible for the management of children with AS. Yes, they are responsible for their learning. Who, though, is going to help these children in their struggle along the social path through school? How may they be helped through the maze of sensory, social and communicative challenges that they face?

This book is about solutions. It starts off at home, with solutions to the problems of school that parents may start to put into practice straightaway. It moves on to suggestions about what parents can help to achieve in the classroom setting, and ends with suggestions for giving whole-school support. It includes, finally, a 'quick reference' section on what to do if and when things go wrong.

School can be a confusing place for children with AS. With its stimulating sensory impact, its socially determined rules and its many apparent inconsistencies it is not the environment which springs to mind when you think what is best for the person with AS. However, despite all of its drawbacks, school can be made to make sense. For it to do so, the various members of the team –

school, child and parents – need to work together, to understand each other's point of view and each accept the idiosyncrasies of the others. I hope this book can help to begin this acceptance process.

Note

Throughout the book I use 'him' to refer to a child with AS and 'her' to refer to the teacher, but this is purely for clarity. It in no way suggests that girls with AS are in any way less important or less to be included, nor that male teachers are less able to adapt!

1

Where Do We Start? What You Can Do by Yourself as Parent(s)

Many parents feel 'left out of the loop' when it comes to the schooling of their child with Asperger syndrome (AS). Perhaps they feel inadequate to make suggestions, or that any suggestions they make are not listened to. Perhaps they are put off by the acronyms and jargon which have sprung up around education. Perhaps they feel that school has changed so much since their school days that they no longer know what to expect.

The most useful suggestions made to me by the parents of schoolchildren with AS, are concerned with breaking down the perceived barrier between home and school. Although many parents admit that they felt it was there, they also admit that once they confronted the barrier, it disappeared. Once they got over their reticence about getting involved in their child's experience of school, things improved radically. The best stories are ones where the parents and school staff work together to understand and accommodate the child's AS. It can be done.

Undoubtedly, the place to start is with the parent(s) themselves. The suggestions in this chapter are all concerned with things that you can do now, straightaway, and without having to make many great requests of the school. On the whole, they are all things that open the school experience up, and which – once implemented – give parents both more access to the school life of their child, and more confidence to influence it. They are an excellent place to start!

1.1 Get involved

The best way to bridge the gap between your child's home life and his life at school is to be that bridge yourself. If you are in school, you will get to know the members of staff as people, and they will be able to see your level of concern and commitment. Working together puts you in the position of adults together, all pulling in the same direction to help your child. Most schools for the age-range covered by this book (four- to ten-year-olds) welcome parent input. You could go in to hear children read or you could go along as a parent helper on school trips. You could apply to be a lunchtime supervisor (that's a 'dinner lady' in old-fashioned terms). Do not imply that some jobs are beneath you. I am a teacher, but I have worked as a lunchtime supervisor, and I learnt as much about that school from that job as I did from my more formal position. Get involved in the Parent–Teacher Association (PTA), help with fund-raising, run a stall at the Summer Fête. Even if you work full-time, there are ways to become involved, even if it means taking some of your holidays to do so. The more you give, the more the school is likely to trust and accept your requests. You are no longer sitting back as 'consumer' of the school's services, expecting it to deliver and complaining when it does not. By getting involved you are working together – and you are in a position to understand just how hard, just how time-consuming and exhausting, teaching is as a profession. In my experience, the parents who complain are seldom the parents who know a school from the inside. You will understand which of your requests are reasonable, and which are things you are better doing for yourself, when you become part of your child's school world.

You will also find that you get to know the teachers as individuals, and have a far greater appreciation of who to go to for specific help. Teachers, like us all, have individual interests and strengths. You may find that Mr G of Class 6 has the kind of confident teaching style that you know will mean that your child can opt for after-school sport with him with a good chance of success, or that Miss J is a computer expert who would be only too happy to give you advice on word-prediction software. Schools are communities, and they can only really be understood from the inside. If you are going to help your child pick his way through this volatile social environment, it is as well to understand its intricacies yourself.

By getting involved you can help out. During the school play someone is always needed to put out chairs, to help with make-up, sell raffle tickets and wash up the coffee cups. By helping where you are needed you are building up a bank of goodwill – from the school as an entity and from individual teachers and support staff. You are putting yourself into a position where your requests are likely to be listened to and considered.

Just as important, by being there you will start to understand the demands and strengths of school as they are experienced by your child. Most of us have strong feelings about school, feelings formed when we were pupils many years ago. What we often do not appreciate is how much schools and education have changed in that time. If we are to be equal partners in ensuring the best education for our children, we need to make sure that we are aware of what school is like now, in the twenty-first century. Only then will we be in a position to advise, to help and to support our children with AS as they negotiate this demanding environment.

Finally, by being there you have a shared reference point with your child. Any parent will know that the question 'What did you do at school today?' is likely to be met by a shrug and the response, 'Nothing.' Our children with AS are even less likely than their neurotypical peers to be able to describe their day to us. If we were there – even for some of the time – we know there was a fire practice, or we know that Mrs S's class was doing assembly, or we know that it was a wet break-time and the children did not go out: we are far more likely to have reference points to access our child's day. Children with AS require specifics. We need to have a grasp of some of the facts of the day before we can even begin to share our child's day with him. Without these points of reference, dropping our child with AS into school is like dropping a pebble into a deep, still pond. We may see the ripples, but we are also quite likely to lose the pebble.

1.2 Provide organization help for your child

Once you understand the demands made on your child in the typical school day, you are in a position to come up with practical suggestions of ways to help. All children at this age need help staying on top of the day-to-day clutter produced by the day at school. They need to be helped by going through their bookbags, extracting letters home, checking pencil cases and sharpening pencils, straightening and checking outdoor wear and finding homework. A child with AS is the same – just more so! Dr Tony Attwood, who wrote the Foreword to this book, has described the need for what he terms an 'Executive Secretary' to steer the child with AS through each day. That job, almost inevitably, is going to fall to the parents. Perhaps you could help the child stay organized by making sure each evening that the previous day's work is finished and that the new day's date is written at the top of the next page. Covering his different books in different-coloured paper may help him to find what he needs quickly. You could provide a folder to put any letters or notices home into, and that members of staff may check to see if you have sent in any replies. Sometimes practical help may be as simple as bringing his sports kit home, turning it all back the right way out, pairing the socks together and untying shoelaces. There is a great deal that can be done in practical terms to minimize the confusion and frustration of getting through the day for your child. How you help him to be organized will vary according to what he is doing, and what expectations are made of him, but it is likely that anything you can do in this area is going to help to lessen his stress and help him to achieve.

This constant, daily organizational help may be a benefit, too, in helping your child to organize his week. You will become familiar with homework expectations and schedules, and can help your child to organize time, space and materials to get this done. You will also become sensitive to changes in him through the week. Does he always come home more distressed on Wednesdays? Does he leave his lunch on Thursdays? Are these days when he has music? Are these times when his class teacher is away and so a support teacher takes him? Are they when he has to move classrooms? Your ability to tune into the rhythms of his week will be a great start to identifying where problem spots may be, and will be a start in trying to sort them out.

1.3 Make the school aware of your child's home-based strengths

One of the most important tasks ahead of you is maintaining the self-esteem of your child with AS in school. School can be a place of hard knocks. He may become aware that he is different from other children, that his writing is untidier, that he cannot kick a ball straight, that he cannot stay on the balance beam as well as the others can. Children are in the business of comparing themselves with each other as they struggle to find their own place in the world. Your child with AS may not naturally make these social comparisons in the same way as a neurotypical child might, but that does not stop all the neurotypical children from drawing his attention to his differences. According to Tony Attwood, it is usually somewhere around the age of seven that a child with AS becomes aware that he is different, and this can be a very vulnerable time.

'Being different is just as good as being like everyone else,' says Gunnilla Gerland[1] (2000, p.46), a writer who has AS herself. It is important that you provide examples of what your son *can* do to combat all the things he may find that he *cannot* do as well as his peers. This is no time for modesty. If he is a prolific reader, send him in with an impressive tome and let the other kids see that he is reading way beyond his years. If he builds exquisite models, bring one in for 'Show and Tell'. Engage your child's teacher's help in this. She is unlikely to be aware of his strengths outside school unless you make her aware of them. Once she is in the know, she is in a position to use your child's strengths to raise his profile in the class. She might stage a quiz where one of the subject areas happens to be your son's special interest. Suddenly he is the most valued member of the team. Or she might set a challenge that whichever table learns most spellings in a week gets a special privilege. Again, your son's table is far more likely to appreciate his gift for spelling if the pupils see that not only does the teacher value his achievements, but that they can all benefit from them. Most teachers are past-masters at this sort of social inclusion, but your child's teacher can only do this if she is given the ammunition to use on your child's behalf. Make sure you do!

---

1   Gerland, G. (2000) *Finding Out About Asperger's Syndrome, High-Functioning Autism and PDD*. London: Jessica Kingsley Publishers.

1.4 Make the teacher aware of what motivates your child

It is important also that you make your child's teacher aware of what motivates your son. Whilst neurotypical children may be motivated by a wish to please the teacher, or to have a star to take home to show a parent, these may be meaningless to the child with AS. One of the hardest things with a child with AS is to come up with a motivating factor. As his parents, you know what he likes doing. It may be that this can be transferred into school (if, for example, he is likely to be motivated by the chance to spend ten minutes drawing robots, or to have a chance to spend some time with his card collection). However, if it isn't, you can opt instead for a token system. Perhaps he has to earn five tokens in a day to earn himself a chance to play a certain computer game that evening, or to earn a certain food for tea. You could, perhaps, supply a box of tokens with various rewards (agreed with your child) printed on them, and then he, you and his teacher may negotiate what he has to achieve in order to choose a token. By providing these incentives you are arming the teacher with ways to motivate your child which are meaningful to him. The combination of good motivation and playing to his strengths is a powerful one.

1.5 Form a group with other parents of pupils with AS – within school or in your area

One of the biggest problems facing us, as parents of children with AS, is our isolation. We may feel that we are the only ones facing this situation, and that we have to fight each battle alone. In fact, statistically, there is a very good chance that there will be other children with a diagnosis of AS in most schools. Depending on how open you or the school are about such matters, it is quite likely that other children's parents are as unaware of you as you are of them. The teachers will realize that the children share a common diagnosis, but because of confidentiality, they will not be able to share that information.

One answer is to approach the headteacher or principal and say that you are trying to get in touch with all the other parents of children with AS in the school. You could perhaps prepare a flyer that you can ask her to pass on to the other parents. The headteacher may do this without betraying anyone's confidentiality, and having passed on the information, parents may contact you themselves. It is most helpful if this is done by the school (*see* section 3.12), but even without official support you may still form a group. Indeed, you can spread your net wider and contact other schools in your area, forming a parent support group for your whole community. This support will give you a chance to have a far stronger voice, to share concerns and solutions, and to beat the feeling that you are on your own. Of course the children will differ hugely in their needs. No two children, even sharing the same diagnosis, will display the same symptoms or have the same needs. That said, there will be common issues, and as a group you are in a stronger position to share the challenges of meeting these common needs with the school or schools involved.

1.6 Involve specialists

As part of the process of gaining a diagnosis, and of continuing care, you are likely to see a variety of specialists with your child. These might include paediatricians, speech and language therapists, occupational therapists, play therapists, and so on. Each of these will be, in their own way, an expert in AS, and although they may not be directly related to education, their knowledge and their input could have great significance within a school setting. One of the problems facing us as parents of a child with AS is juggling all the different agencies and their different perspectives. The answer may well be to bring them together yourself.

Members of staff in schools are usually aware of their lack of specialist knowledge, and are keen to learn more. Specialists may be frustrated that what they know does not get carried out in schools. Ask that the next appointment with the specialist takes place in school. Invite the specialist along to talk to your child's teacher. Invite your child's teacher out to the specialist's appointment. You will probably run into consternation as the various agencies tie themselves in knots wondering which budget your son's care should come from if it crosses boundaries in this way. *Don't* let that put you off. Your child is an individual. He does not divide his Asperger difficulties up into areas labelled 'medical', 'educational' and 'social'. Joined-up care may confuse the authorities, but if it is better for your son you should not let their confusion stop you.

1.7 Share responsibility for your child's learning

Many parents' despair comes from the fact that they are aware that their child with AS is not learning at school. We may well have had cognitive tests done on our children as part of the diagnosis process. We may be ultra-knowledgeable about just how intellectually able our child is, yet we remain helpless as we fail to see this potential translated into academic learning. It does not matter where our child falls on the IQ scale. It is quite likely that, however low or high, his academic achievement falls short of his intellectual potential.

Schools are social environments. Much of the learning that takes place in schools is socially based – yet our children have a deficit in social processing. The environment may be alien to our child, so that this in itself provides a barrier to learning. Problems with the semantics of language, and of aural processing generally, may mean that much of what is taught in school bypasses our children. Quite simply, the way in which many children with AS learn is not always the way in which mainstream education is taught.

Understandably, this makes parents angry. It makes teachers unhappy and possibly defensive: it can be very hard when you are teaching to the best of your ability, and the child still fails to learn. Most worryingly, it can make the child with AS feel a failure. Everyone else 'gets' what is going on. The child with AS does not so he deduces he must be stupid. It is flawed logic, but it is understandable.

Parents may feel inadequate in the face of their child's inability to learn, but often they are the best people to help. Yes, schools should and will help. Yes, the Special Educational Needs Co-ordinator (SENCO) or special educational team will become involved, and the teaching assistant or teaching aide (TA), if there is one, will give support. However, the only people who *really* know that child, and who are going to stay the course right through the years until adulthood and beyond, are his parents. Parents must not be made to feel inadequately placed to help their child learn. They may well be the very best teachers for that child.

Most parents are not trained teachers, but then teachers may not have had much training in how a child with AS learns. The person who will know best how he learns is the child himself (although he is unlikely to be aware of it or be able to express it). The parents have the time to spend with that child, to observe him, to learn how he learns and to help him build on his strengths. Parents share the motivation to really tune into their child, to know how to support him in what he can do well and where to help him in areas where he is not so competent. If this learning at home is supported and encouraged by the teacher, so that the school provides resources and current educational practices are shared (children do not learn long division in school these days in the way we did in the 1970s), so much the better. Here is another example of school and home working together to bridge the gap and help the child with AS to achieve.

For example, a child with AS may be a prolific reader. He may be reading, already way beyond his peers, especially books about his current special interest. He is able to absorb, to categorize, to remember and recall vast amounts of information from what he has read. Clearly, he is able to learn in this context. What he needs is the time to do this, a good selection of books from which to learn, the opportunity to widen his reading and therefore learning, and encouragement to view his achievements as worthwhile. All of these can be achieved by a parent just as easily as by a teacher. If the books he reads are around the topics covered at school, so much the better. He may be proficient on the computer. Perhaps he needs greater access to this than the school can provide. Perhaps, given access to a structured distance-learning course, he could in effect educate himself. Parents are in a position to recognize this, and to support their child in his learning. Experts have long recognized that 'asocial' learning (learning that does not rely on a social context) can be ideal for students with AS. Without parental intervention it is unlikely that the child will have sufficient access to this type of learning routinely in school. If the computer program is one recommended by the school and perhaps already used there in the limited time available, this helps the child with AS to learn alongside his peers while acknowledging that he learns differently.

There are likely to be problems too. Perhaps your child struggles to write. This may be a motor problem, a spatial processing problem, letter-recognition deficit, phonetic processing problems – any number of reasons. As parents, you are in a position to investigate just what is going on, and to call in expert help as needed. You are also in a position to give your child the one-to-one support many remedial programmes demand, and at the level he needs rather than at the level at which the school can fund. Parents of children with disabilities the world over have fought against the limitations imposed on their children by society. Parents have taught children who 'would never walk' to climb mountains, who 'would never speak' to sing. Parents have taught everything from how to dress, wash, live independently, read, write, handle money, tell the time. Parents should never feel that only teachers have the expertise to teach their child. A good teacher, aware of her own time and skill limitations, will welcome all the parental input she can get, and will support that learning with ideas, resources and encouragement. The point is that the child with AS should be supported to learn. Who facilitates that learning is a minor consideration.

Of course, it may be that your child is arriving home from school exhausted by having to negotiate an alien environment all day. It may be that he is simply too tired to learn with you at that time. Talk to your child's headteacher. It may well be possible to negotiate a 'flexi-school' arrangement. Perhaps your son could go to school in the mornings only, or perhaps he could have a day off in the week where you can operate an alternative learning programme for him, agreed with the school. Such ideas are innovative, and they require a flexible and enlightened approach from all the adults involved. However, there is nothing to stop you trying for whatever system works best for your child. Don't settle for the 'norm'. The norm is just that: the usual for the typical child. Your child is different and has different needs. It may take a totally individual, tailored approach to best meet his needs, and if so, that is well worth fighting for.

1.8 Be involved fully in reviews

Because your child has special educational needs, at whatever level the school recognizes these to be, you are likely to be asked to come into school to 'review' his progress. These reviews can seem fairly intimidating, seeming as they do to carry all the school's authority behind them. It is important that you do not let them have this effect. In fact, these are your opportunity formally to influence your child's educational provision. It is for you to take the initiative.

It helps, in any meeting, if all parties are clear what the agenda of that meeting will be. When you receive notification that there is to be a review of your child's progress, clarify who will be there and what topics the various professionals want to cover. Add your own concerns and, if possible, get all the subjects to be covered put in writing. Everyone in school is always short of time. The clearer you can be about what is to be discussed, the more will get covered by everyone.

If, during the course of the meeting, any issues arise which you feel do not get adequately resolved, ask for clarity about what the next move will be on this subject and what the timescale will be. It may be that a matter needs to be discussed with the headteacher. It may be that a report from an outside professional is required before further action may be taken. Whatever it is that is slowing down progress, get clear information about what the next move will be and when you can hope to hear that it has happened. This is not to suggest any hostility, but merely to recognize that schools are busy places and that other priorities may take over if you do not stay clearly focussed on the specifics of your child's case. Ask that all decisions about what will happen next are recorded in minutes of the meeting and that you have a copy. This may all seem rather officious if you know the members of staff involved well and have a good working relationship with them, but in fact it is merely being professional and recognizing their professional involvement.

If some matters are not resolved to your satisfaction, or if you run out of time, make further appointments. You can ask to make an appointment with another member of staff or with the headteacher. Try not to get angry if you feel you are not getting anywhere. Keep what you want for your child clear in your mind, and keep the reasons why you want it clear also. Work towards what is best for your child, and keep believing that the professionals in school want what is best for him too. Although you may sometimes feel beleaguered, you are all in fact on the 'same side', working towards a common goal. It can help to keep this consciously in mind.

If you really do feel that you have hit a brick wall, it is as well to familiarize yourself with law and current legislation. School may be familiar with legislation relating to education, but they may not be so familiar with it relating to disability. Do not assume that school professionals will be up to date with all the latest policies and guidelines. They are, primarily, teachers, not lawyers. It may be for you to dig into the law on their behalf, and indeed check out their rights as much as your child's.

1.9 Share home or school information

Sharing information between home and school is probably the most important element of all in maintaining your child's welfare. After all, this is, fundamentally, communication. If you know what your child has done, felt, experienced, learnt, said at school – and if your child's teachers know the same about his out-of-school life – there is every chance that he will experience real understanding and genuine, individually tailored education. But how do we manage this?

One forum is the home–school diary. This is simply a small notebook that travels between home and school each day with your child, and which makes communication easier. You can use it to alert school staff to differences in your child (i.e. a disturbed night's sleep, bad news in the family) and also to bring your child's home-based strengths and successes to the school's attention. It is a quick way to clarify information that your child may find difficult to convey. One of the problems with AS is that the child may be unable to give contextual references in what he says, and therefore someone who was not there may really struggle to understand what he is reporting. Work with your child on this; explain that you have written the outline of what you did over the weekend, and that he is to give the book to his teacher before he tries to describe it himself.

To work, a diary needs to be more than a cheerful record of a 'good day', as commonly seen at nursery age. Think about specifics: work with your son's teacher or TA to target one thing at a time. For instance, if the school has been concerned about his behaviour in the lunch line, work just on that. Find out specifics: what is happening, what is your child doing, how are pupils and staff reacting, what does your son have to say on the matter, are there any simple practical solutions (like allowing him to line up at the back). For the book to be effective it has to report the negative as well as the positive. It is, curiously, most effective when school staff are able to admit that they do not know what to do, and to ask the parents for advice – and vice versa. Bear in mind that this relationship requires trust, and will not happen overnight.

Some parents, particularly those who are sensitive about their own level of literacy, may find a home–school diary intimidating. If so, don't use one! Communication is not made better if one party feels at a disadvantage to another. If you feel happier talking face to face then that is the best way to communicate. Open access to chat with your child's teacher before and after each session is the ideal, but few teachers will have the time or be willing to do this. (Some will, and are wonderful, but it cannot be taken as the norm.) Perhaps you will be blessed with a TA who has time to operate this feedback, but, again, this may be a matter of chance unless you formalize the arrangement (*see* section 2.3). The problem is that your child, because of his AS, has a deficit in social communication. By definition he is unlikely to enable this information exchange himself. The typically functioning child goes home, perhaps cries, tells his mother if he has been in trouble, pushed in the playground or lost his reading book. The typically functioning child may be able to explain to his teacher that he has not completed his homework because he was at hospital all evening visiting his sick granny. The child with AS may well struggle in these sort of exchanges. He may struggle with 'Where were you last evening?' so it is pretty certain that he is not going to be able to give the information if faced with 'Why haven't you done your homework?' If the teacher does not know what question to ask, there is little chance of getting a useful answer. The same is true about home questions about school. If you know to ask, 'Did Mark kick you today?' you may get an answer, but 'Did you have a good day?' is unlikely to get to the bottom of what is really going on.

At its simplest, it is this lack of social communication ability that makes your child most vulnerable in school. You are going to have to overcome this deficit yourself. One way, as outlined earlier, is to get involved in school as much as possible, even when other parents no longer do so. It may be that, as parents of typically functioning children, it is healthy to give children space as they grow up, and to back out of their private life as they get older. Not knowing all that goes on at school is a healthy step towards this – if the child is typically functioning. If the child has AS, this backing off is more problematic, and however overprotective or irritatingly 'always there' it might make us seem, we are going to have to keep the lines of communication open ourselves. By being there we may, in fact, help our child take practical steps towards successful independence. We may have to be inventive, and we may have to adapt to each new teacher, but we should stick in there. Ultimately, if we do not know what is going on then we cannot help, and if the teacher does not know then neither can she.

As electronic notebooks become more common – and more reasonably priced – these may well be a way forward to replace the paper notebook for communication. The electronic notebook can be programmed with schedules, timetables, cues and reminders, and may be accessed by members of staff, by parents and by the pupil himself. Best of all, this is a socially acceptable 'adult' device. Many people I know can no longer function without their electronic notebook! The reason this is important is that it is using a solution that will travel with your son into adulthood. We should aim, always, for ways to help our children towards increased independence and for ways to help them to manage their AS for themselves.

1.10 Find out about visits (both to school and out of school)

One area where problems can occur is when the usual routine of school is disrupted, either by a visit of a group to the school, or a visit by the pupils out of school.

If a group is coming into school (perhaps a theatre company is coming in to perform a play about road safety), it is important that the school gives you plenty of warning so that you can go through the possible issues with your son. He will need to be reminded about the 'rules' of watching a play, and you will need to be sure he is confident about the content, especially if is likely to involve difficult choices or any degree of peril. The child with AS may be far more sensitive to what happens on stage than his neurotypical peers. He may find the concept that the actors are 'just pretending' difficult to accept, and he may get more caught up in the drama than the rest of the class. What is entirely appropriate to the age group at which the play is aimed may not be appropriate for the child with AS, who may be emotionally very immature. If you are unsure whether the visit is appropriate for your child, ask if you could go in and watch the play with him, or request that he be withdrawn from the activity. You may even collect him and take him home.

Visits out by pupils to off-school venues can involve additional problems, as well as those mentioned above. You will want, first of all, to decide whether the trip is appropriate for your son, and whether he will get anything out of it. If you decide that it is suitable, and that he would benefit from going, then you will need to reassure yourself, at very least, that he will be physically safe and that he will not get lost. In addition, will your child need support to understand what is being asked of him? Will he need help with practical matters like choosing or eating food in a strange environment, or accessing the bathroom? If your son has a TA, you can ask if she may be allocated to go on the trip as part of her hours, and discuss your concerns with her. If your child does not have a teaching aide, then ultimately these concerns may mean that you need to go along on the trip as a parent helper. If you are unable to be there yourself and remain concerned about your son, there is nothing to stop you working with the school to have a private arrangement with someone to go along as an unofficial TA on this occasion. You might ask a family friend or another parent. It is, of course, the school's responsibility to make sure that your child is safe on these trips, but if you are concerned it may be best to come up with this sort of pragmatic solution. If it means your child may go on the trip and be safe, and that you do not worry, it is probably not such a high price to pay.

1.11 Discuss the issue of homework

Homework can be a real problem for a child with AS. He may just about be managing to get through the day, knowing he can return to the safe haven of home at the end of it. He may find it very difficult indeed if he is then expected to bring work from school and to 'contaminate' his home environment with it. As parents, we may find ourselves coping with the fall-out from this, with the meltdowns and the tears, and we may find ourselves doing his homework for him. At some point, everyone needs to step off this pointless roundabout and take a look at what is supposed to be achieved by it all.

First of all, you need to ask your child's class teacher if homework is really necessary. It may be school policy, but often this is not because the school is particularly keen on it, but because some parents demand it. If your child does not do homework, is anyone really going to notice or mind?

If the policy is that homework has to be done, you could perhaps negotiate a time in school when your child could tackle it. If he is struggling with the unstructured time of breaks (*see* section 2.5), perhaps a member of staff would be willing to run a lunchtime homework club, and your son could get the work done then. Does his homework need to be exactly the same as everyone else's? The class teacher is probably already giving differentiated tasks to accommodate the different learning needs of the pupils. Perhaps your son's 'homework' could be something he does already – perhaps it could be to read a school book as part of his bedtime reading, or to use an educational CD-ROM and achieve a certain level by the end of the week.

The problem of homework can be dealt with if it is met head on. It is worth facing up to, though. Homework is likely to become a bigger problem as your son gets older if you do not find a way of confronting it now. Pupils are given homework because they are expected to be able to work and to learn independently as they move up the school. *Working* independently and *learning* independently are not the same things. Your son may need considerable support in his work, which may make home*work* a considerable trial (for you all), yet be only too happy to *learn* independently at home. In fact, if independent learning is what is required, the child with AS is probably well ahead of his peers already. Your child has different needs because of his AS. Do not be afraid to make that point, and defend him against doing something just because it is what is expected of everyone else. You son has AS. Does he really need homework?

1.12 Provide continuity during holiday times

Conversely, having said what I just have about homework, there is a time when introducing an element of schoolwork to home may be a good idea. This might happen during holiday periods, when your child may get out of routines established in school, and may even miss the structure they provide. Having a daily timetable during the otherwise unstructured school holidays may be very reassuring for some children with AS. You could, for example, introduce the idea of formal reading time during the morning, or the routine writing of a diary for half an hour before bed. This might be a good time to introduce the idea of a holiday project, with research, writing and presentation of ideas. If your son is struggling with one area of the curriculum, for example with writing, holiday time is a good opportunity to provide support, perhaps by encouraging him to follow an online typing or word-processing course. Having some formal 'work' to share with your child can be a great way of interacting with him, and may provide opportunities for social interaction and shared interests with you and his siblings. If the idea is presented in a positive way, some formal educational work during the holidays need not be the nightmare it at first sounds!

1.13 Invite members of staff home, especially the class teacher

Even as I write this seems a revolutionary concept, and may appear even more so depending on where you, the readers, live. A generation or two ago, the teacher might have been a well-known person in your town, and you might very well have invited her round to dinner as a matter of courtesy without any thought about whether it would help your child at school. Now, teachers in most places are highly unlikely to ever visit a child's home. In many places it would be considered inappropriate, or even dangerous, to do so.

We have lost a great deal through this. As part of the process of diagnosing AS in our son, a number of health professionals visited him to see him in his home context. These included researchers, nurses, health visitors and psychologists, and very reassuring it was, too. Having visited our son at home, they understood him and his home environment better.

Teachers do not have access to this information. They see our child, and us, in only one context, and this context is of their making, not ours. To most (although not all) neurotypical children this will not matter much, since they are quick to accept that school has a culture all of its own. To a child with AS, though, the discrepancies in social rules between home and school may be very serious. If the difference in rules is not understood, how can the child hope to adapt?

Children with AS come from all socio-economic backgrounds, all ethnic, religious and cultural groups. It is quite possible, therefore, that the prevailing social culture of home may well not be that of school nor necessarily that of many of the other children in the class, nor of the teacher, headteacher or TA. Yet the child with AS (who, by definition of diagnosis, finds adapting to meet different social contexts a challenge) is the one who is expected to adapt to the different social rules. The teacher or other professional (who has no diagnosed difficulty in adapting) is the one who dictates the social environment. It really does not make sense.

Asking professionals from school to visit your child's home environment may raise eyebrows, but that does not mean it is not a good idea for the welfare of the child. In an ideal world, the education of your child will span both home and school environments. As suggested earlier, it is likely to help if you take home into school. It is not unreasonable also to ask to bring school into your home.

1.14 Be aware of the school's anti-bullying policies, and be prepared to become involved quickly if issues arise

Bullying is serious, and, unfortunately, children with AS are particularly vulnerable to it. The best thing that you can do as a parent is to be confident that you can deal with bullying if and when it occurs. Do not wait and hope it will not happen. Of course it may not, but if you are prepared in advance and confident that you can do something to help, you are far more likely to be in a position to deal with the problems of bullying quickly and efficiently, and before too much damage is done. Many adolescents with AS experience depression, often caused by aspects of bullying (either active – violence, name-calling, 'teasing' or passive – being left out, isolated, ignored) at school. The threat of bullying needs to be taken very seriously indeed.

Schools should have an anti-bullying policy, and it is best if you make yourself thoroughly familiar with this right from the start.

That way you will know immediately what to do, who to approach and what actions to request as soon as you have any suspicion that bullying is taking place. Be aware your child's social communication deficit is likely to make him less able to articulate that he is being bullied, so you are going to have to be extra-vigilant. You need also to be aware (as does the school) that your child's sensory differences may mean that he feels bullied by behaviour that would not seem serious to someone else, and that he may feel so even if this was not the intention. A light push, or a playful tickle, which may be seen as friendly to a neurotypical child, may be intrusive, painful or frightening for a child with AS.

Although rare, bullying by an adult can happen to a child in school. If any adult refuses to compensate for your child's AS, this could be described as bullying and is likely to be illegal under disability discrimination law. For example, an adult might insist that your son line up near where the bell for change of lessons goes off even though his auditory sensitivity makes this painful. Or she might demand that he go in to change his shoes in the busy cloakroom even though the jostling and claustrophobia induced by so many people is distressing for him. Or she might insist that he take his turn to read aloud to the class even though his anxiety levels are massively raised. Each of these is an example of occasions when understanding of AS may be limited, and where awareness of AS needs to be improved. However, if the adult has been made aware, yet refuses to understand or to compensate, then the school authorities need to be involved and both the anti-bullying policy and disability discrimination law cited. Fortunately, the vast majority of incidents such as these are attributed to misunderstanding of the condition of AS, and not to malice. The days when all children, regardless of differences, were expected to 'knuckle under' and put up with things are, thankfully, in the past. This is a battle that has already been won. If you find yourself fighting it, you would probably be wise to seek legal advice.

2

Looking for Help Within the Classroom

The people who are going to have the greatest influence on how your child manages school are going to be his teachers and, if he has one, his teaching assistant or teaching aide (TA). Parents tend to be reticent about making suggestions to these professionals, and with good reason. These people are precisely that: professionals, and no one takes kindly to having their professionalism questioned nor to having an outsider tell them what to do. The way that you as a parent of a child with AS approach this will have to be diplomatic. It must be clear that you are not criticizing the teacher's working practices, nor implying that you know better than she does how to teach your child. What you are doing is providing support for your child, and acknowledging that his needs are different from those of the rest of the class. You will need to make it clear that it is your child's needs that are different (and you are not, therefore, questioning the teacher's working with any other pupils), and that it is him that you see as needing the support (not the teacher). With luck and a persistent, diplomatic approach it should be possible for you and your child's class teacher to work together. Both of you should come to realize that by sharing his care and education, and by dovetailing it so that these are consistent across the different parts of his day, you are working together to do the best for your child.

Indeed, most teachers will probably welcome your input. In the course of discussions for this book, many teachers have expressed their frustration that parents have a 'stop at the door' attitude which precludes greater involvement. Both teachers and teaching assistants have been puzzled by the fact that it is often extremely difficult to get parents to take an active, equal role in the care of their child during school hours. If your child has support time allocated to him by a TA, then she is the ideal person to facilitate this 'dovetailing', and to provide the consistency for your son and the communication between you and his teacher which is so valuable. You will need to make sure that the teaching assistant has the time to do this, and that it is made clear that you expect to be part of deciding how her allocated hours should be spent (*see* section 2.3). Even if your child has not been allocated TA support, you and his class teacher can still work together to make sure that what you both do in the different parts of his life is consistent. As long as both you and your child's teacher believe that his interests come first, there is every chance that you can forge a good working relationship.

2.1 Talk to the teacher about classroom look and layout

As your relationship with your child's class teacher grows, and as your familiarity with the classroom and how the various parts of it are used during the day and week grows, you will be in a position to discuss classroom layout. Be aware that classroom layout is often highly individual to that teacher. What may appear random or inconvenient to you will be there for a very good reason. A teacher of this children's age group will usually have her own classroom base (with older pupils it may be the teacher who is more likely to move around the school to teach different age groups) and her classroom will reflect her teaching style. It will also almost definitely reflect the ethos of the school. What the teacher, and indeed the headteacher, may be unaware of, is the degree to which the classroom environment itself may be contributing to the underachievement of a child with AS.

Many primary classrooms are bright, visually stimulating, exciting environments to be in. The walls are covered with bright displays; information leaps from every wall; bright colours abound. Every effort is made to make the room bright and light. The interactive whiteboard shines at the front, computer screens beckon to the side, the fluorescent light whirrs on its frantic cycle, the overhead projector and the air conditioner hum. Children sit, not in straight rows facing the front of the room, but scattered in islands, often in a different place for each activity, frequently with each group doing something different. Conversation and interaction are usually encouraged, as is listening to the teacher. Yet the teacher may be the stillest, least bright object in the room, and what she is saying may have nothing to do with the list of 'our adjectives of the week', each written in a different font of a different colour, which happens to be directly behind her.

The stimulation that works for neurotypical children may be the very thing that confuses and distresses a child with AS. For a child who is a strong visual learner it may be literally impossible to filter out the many exciting stimuli, so that it is these which are repeatedly being absorbed, and the spoken words of the teacher that are lost. Some visual stimuli may be so powerful to the child with AS that they are actually distressing. An example is the technique of double-mounting displays on walls. The white paper on a bright background, with another contrasting bright colour behind that, all mounted on a board which is itself often colourful, and which may have a border, or borders, running around it may be, literally, painful for a child with AS. It may be impossible to filter it out so that he is always aware of it, and is forced to read and re-read the same material again and again.

The zones of a classroom may be confusing, too. The 'book corner' may not actually be in a corner (!), and it may have an invisible area attached to it beyond which you must not cross. It is OK to read a book sitting on the floor, but not OK to carry that same book two steps and sit on a chair. The chair, although there is nothing to indicate this, is not in the book corner, but is indefinably linked to the table at which other children are doing science work. One of the most common oddities in primary school is the invitation to 'Come and sit on the carpet', when the whole room is carpeted. How is the child with AS to make sense of the fact that everyone else seems to know by a process of osmosis that what is meant is 'Sit on the carpet in two rows, facing the same way and within an invisible semicircle of my making'? It is all desperately confusing, and making sense of all of it may be as much as a child with AS can manage. There is little mental energy left for taking in information about the rules on what constitutes a rhombus.

Clearly, although understanding this is a start, it is unrealistic to expect the other 30 or so children to complete their education in a sombre, plain-coloured room, lacking any light or movement, and with every rule rigidly clarified and displayed. Nor is it realistic to expect the teacher to alter teaching techniques which work to inspire the majority of the class, merely because they cause confusion in one individual. What is needed, clearly, is a compromise. Usually, merely being able to discuss the situation is enough. Most teachers will go to extraordinary lengths to accommodate the needs of all their pupils, and once she understands the problems, your child's teacher may well devise new and innovative suggestions. Some that you could add might include having a carpet square for your child specifically to sit on ('his space', but one that can be moved as necessary); swapping chairs with another classroom – if the caretaker will agree – so that the science table has red metal chairs and the craft table has wooden ones; using masking tape to delineate the extremities of the reading area. It may help to have one small area that is display-free, which your child can face to get on with quiet work, and to allow your child to sit near a window and use natural light as opposed to fluorescent lighting. Distraction through the window may be avoided by putting opaque film on the lower part of the window. Most of these are not huge undertakings, and if you are happy to come in and give your time moving tables or chairs, so much the better. You and your child's class teacher working together are likely to be a pretty potent force!

2.2 Provide specifics that already work

In the course of your reading, talking to other parents, attending support groups and lectures or workshops you will come across a huge range of specific supports which have worked with other children with AS in the past. These might include using schedules, written stories, emotion cards, traffic lights to regulate volume, whatever! It is tempting to take each new idea and immediately see it as the solution to all problems ('Of course! If he has a schedule, his level of anxiety is bound to fall…') and to arrive at the school the following morning filled with enthusiasm and expecting the school to implement it straightaway. Realistically, this is unlikely to work. For a start, too many new strategies are just going to confuse your child, and if the various parties are not confident using them they are unlikely to be effective anyway. The result is that the techniques are seen by the school, by you, by your child, not to work, and are abandoned before the good in them may be appreciated.

As ever, you may well be in the best position to introduce and then evaluate the effectiveness of a technique with your child. If, for example, you decide from what you have learnt, that a schedule is a good technique to try for your child (and remember, each child is different: it is possible to end up feeling guilty if you do not try every technique you hear about), it may be best to introduce it slowly and carefully at home. Pick a time of day, for example bedtime, and evaluate how things go with your child over the period of a week to a fortnight. You might have an assessment that includes number of fights with a sibling, length of time taken to get into bed, how many times your child gets back out of bed, how long it takes your child to fall asleep. Include other variables, such as food eaten in the four hours up to bedtime, whether other influences change (e.g. was one parent away on business for some days?) and a general impression of how happy and relaxed your child was each night.

You are then in a position to introduce a schedule. You might go through it with your child and decide what the component parts are in 'going to bed'. These might include taking a bath, changing into pyjamas, brushing teeth, listening to a story, having a reading time, receiving a five-minute warning to lights out, and a goodnight kiss. Make a simple flowchart schedule, showing each component. This needs to have some means of showing that each point has been reached (e.g. being able to remove components and put them into a 'finished' pouch), and to have a clear progression, usually downwards.

Introduce the schedule, and give a period of at least a week to get used to it. Then reassess the night-time routine using the same criteria as before. Does your son fight less with siblings? Is he quicker getting into bed? Does he stay there more consistently, go to sleep quicker? Is he more relaxed and confident at bedtime, knowing what is going to happen and when?

If he is – if you evaluate that this technique works – you may or may not decide to keep it going for bedtimes. The point is that you are now confident that a schedule works to calm your son, and give him more self-assurance about a routine. You are now in a strong position to introduce the concept to school.

In order for the school or class teacher to believe that the extra work needed to introduce the technique is worth it, you need a similar, small-scale challenge. It is unlikely to be a great success if introduced immediately to cover the whole day. Instead, work with your son's teacher or TA to identify one particular trouble spot in the day. It could be the routine for coming in from breaktime, lining up for lunch or getting changed for sport. Work with the school to identify the steps that make up this trouble spot, and break them down. Be prepared to make the schedule yourself, both to minimize the work imposed on school staff at this stage and to provide consistency with the schedule that you know already works.

Be confident when asking that the technique be tried. You have not barged in, expecting the school to change what they are doing with an 'I know a better way' approach. You are introducing a technique suggested by reputable sources, which you have researched with your child and which you have spent time preparing. In this context it is unlikely that you will meet resistance to trying the technique, and it might be argued quite strongly that it would be unacceptable if you did. Be positive – you want the school staff to be enthusiastic about trying it, and to do their best to make it work.

If the technique does work (fingers crossed!) you have given the school something that can be used next time a specific problem area occurs with your child. Even more important, you are giving your child a technique that he can begin to generalize over different contexts. He may need help setting up and implementing this now, while at primary school, but the technique itself can stay with him. He may find that as an adult, he uses a 'checklist' before leaving the house in the morning, or that he builds himself a schedule, mental or written, for checking that he has locked the doors, put out the cat, and so on before going to bed. Anything that works for your child has to be useful for helping him manage his AS throughout his life.

2.3 Be imaginative about TA support

Depending on your child's diagnosis, and on a whole range of other variables too numerous to mention, it may be that he will be offered some TA support. The teaching assistant is an adult whose 'job' for an allocated period of time each week is to work with your child. This adult support can be your most valuable asset. A really good TA may be the most wonderful help for your child. Here is someone who can interpret the world of school for your child, who can support him both academically and socially, who can communicate on his behalf and who is there for him to turn to when things get tough. It is important never to underestimate the huge difference a good TA can make. Quite simply, good TA support may be the difference for a child with AS which 'makes school make sense'.

However, it is important as a parent not to see the provision of some hours of support as being the answer to all problems. Yes, this is a tremendous resource, but for it to work to maximum benefit, your child, the TA and you need to build up a relationship, and need to share open communication. And that is not as easy as you might expect.

It is not usual, for example, for any of the TA's time to be allocated to talking to the child's parents. If you want to communicate with your child's TA, you have to rely on her being willing to stay after hours and give up her time to do so. This really is not fair. TAs are not usually employed on the same professional contracts as teachers, and are paid for the hours they work. Indeed, your child's allocation of support will probably be quoted to you in terms of hours (e.g. '...15 hours a week'). This means that, from the start, communication may be difficult.

The next difficulty may be that the TA works under the direction of your child's teacher, not you. As another adult in the classroom, she may be called upon to do all sorts of duties, not always directly related to your child. This varies tremendously from school to school, but it may occasionally be the case that your child's TA may be asked to work with other children or even in another classroom, on work which has nothing to do with what your child is doing. The thinking behind this can be valid; perhaps by doing this work the TA is freeing up the teacher to give your child extra time. On the other hand, you may start to feel that the support is becoming used to help the teacher, and not to help your child. It is best if you are able to be very clear about what the responsibilities of your child's TA are, and to avoid conflicts of interest before they occur.

It is also the case that, although your child's TA may have had excellent AS-specific training (and there is more of this available at this level than for any other members of staff in schools), it is also quite possible that she will have had no training whatsoever. Again, there is no stipulation that your son's TA should have attained a certain level of education. Depending on the ethos of the school, TAs may be regarded as dedicated professionals who have all kinds of specialist understanding and skills, and who have received all manner of specific training, or they may be treated as little more than unskilled 'minders'. It is for you to fight on behalf of your child, and indeed on behalf of your child's TA, to ensure that the enormous value of what your child's support can do is recognized by all.

A good start in this is to establish right from the beginning how your child's allocated hours are going to be spent. There is nothing wrong with requesting that at least one of these each week is spent with you (although this may have to be during school hours and to include your child). It may be argued that this time is not directly 'supporting' your child, but that is a fallacy. This hour of communication may provide the greatest source of support that your child has. It is not much good if your child's TA goes on training about use of visual prompts, for example, if she does not have a chance to share that training with you. Without communication, nothing which works in school is going to be translated to the home, nor will what works at home be taken across into school. Given that one of the greatest strengths of having a TA is the improvement in communication, time for this needs to be written into the plan. With an allocated time in which to discuss them, problems that occur at school may be dealt with before they escalate. The TA can work with the teacher, with the child and with you to understand what is going wrong, and what to do about it. She should also have time to implement any strategies you all decide to put into place.

For example, earlier we discussed the idea of a schedule. If you have time to go through the thinking behind a schedule with your TA, she is likely to be the best person to implement it in school and to evaluate its success. Similarly, you may all identify break-times as a problem area for your child. Perhaps you can request that some of her allocated hours be given to break-time. The TA then becomes one of the extra adults available to monitor the wildlife garden, or run 'craze of the week' (see section 3.3). What is unfair is to expect her to do this in addition to time directed by the teacher, who might already have plans for her to work with a small group – including your child – on writing a play script. Clearly, you are all going to have to be very clear about what is wanted by all parties.

Similarly, you may feel it would be helpful if your child's TA is present at reviews or at parents' evenings so that she is able to join in discussion about his overall progress. If so, it is important to request this through the school, rather than merely asking the TA herself. Many TAs give much more than their allocated time to best provide care for their charges and their contribution is not always as valued as it should be by the school authorities. As a parent, you may have far more 'clout' than your son's TA, so it is important that you make clear that she is a valued member of the team and should be treated professionally.

Equally, if you are not happy that your son's TA has sufficient understanding of AS you are in a position to request that she go for training. Find courses, enrol yourself and then request that she be given time to attend as well. This proactive approach may cause a few raised eyebrows, but most schools are aware that they should increase their levels of AS training. By offering training opportunities to a member of staff you are ultimately offering an improvement to the school, and not just for your child. Again, you may be in a stronger position as a parent to request this training than the TA is herself. Having received training, your TA is in a stronger position to offer suggestions and solutions to ways of managing your child's AS issues. All in all, it leads to greater AS awareness all round.

2.4 Provide or suggest a whole range of visual cues and clues

It may be that you know your child responds to visual cues. Perhaps you already use an 'angry card' (a card that he can present instead of lashing out and which is always taken seriously) or a star chart to reinforce behaviour, or a tick chart to organize what to take with him to school in the morning. Perhaps you use written stories with your child to explain social situations that he finds difficult. If these work for your child, it makes sense to bring them into school (although not all at once). Most of these devices are ready-made for classroom use. Perhaps all that is needed is that your child's teacher is made aware of how powerful these tools are with your child for her to incorporate them into his school day.

What is imperative is that techniques are consistent across the two environments. For example, if you have introduced an 'angry card' system at home, and through its use eliminated any lashing out by your child at his sister, the same technique if brought into school *must* be respected. If your son remembers to present his angry card to a lunchtime supervisor rather than lashing out at a tormentor, it is worse than useless if she has no idea what it is or what it means (*see* Chapter 3). Similarly, if putting a piece of work into the 'Finished Tray' at school means that no further work need be done on it during that session, you need to be aware of this and to have, and respect, a 'finished tray' at home for homework.

In fact, schools are often very good at visual cues. They may already have a 'Voices Down' or 'Quiet Working' sign that is put up to remind all pupils, or perhaps a timetable of the day that is displayed at the front of the class at the beginning of the morning. In fact, if you are able to go into school and see them in action, there may be any manner of such cues that you might decide to adapt and use at home. Consistency across home and school environments can work both ways, and a 'Wait' card or a 'Five-minute warning to change of activity' token could be useful in all sorts of home situations.

Remember that you and your child's teacher are working always towards greater independence for your child. If these sorts of visual cues work for him, work with him on suggesting and making them himself. Many of us start a busy day or a difficult task by making a list or a plan. Many of us post notes and reminders on the fridge or around our computer screens. There is nothing to say that visual cues need be AS-specific or even child-specific. If each of us who shares our life with someone with AS could get used to indicating our intentions and our expectations visually it would probably be better and easier for us all.

2.5 Ask that break-time rules be made explicit

Break-time may be one of the hardest parts of the school day for a pupil with AS, yet it is often the time when there is least supervision or support. During lesson times there are rules, and at least someone is in charge to try to ensure that there is relative quiet, consistency and order. At break-time everyone runs outside and darts about apparently at random. There are no rules, it is noisy, there is constant movement and no one seems to be in charge. Yet there are rules, even if the person with AS does not understand them. There are highly structured inferred social rules at work at break-time, and these may be most confusing of all. Far from being a time to let off steam and relax, break-time for the pupil with AS may be the time in the day of greatest stress.

There is much the school can do to help with this (*see* section 3.3). If techniques have not been established there is much that the class teacher and TA can do to help in the meantime. One of the simplest ways is to get the class to agree, and then display, some simple playground rules. As a parent, it is reasonable to ask for this, or at least to request that the rules be made clear to you so that you can explain them to your child. In trying to explain the rules to you, the teacher or TA may become aware of just how amorphous the rules are, and that may be a help in itself. If the adults have not formalized what is allowed and what is not, how can the children be expected to know?

When asking the adults to articulate the rules, try to persuade them to do so in positives rather than negatives. It is not much use to tell a child with AS not to walk across the football pitch. It does not stop him running across it, sitting down in the middle of it or playing on the edge of it! What is of more use is a rule saying that to get to the far side of the pitch it is a rule to walk around the white line. Similarly, instructions not to push when in line are not as helpful as those saying how to line up, what distance to leave between you and the person in front and what to do with your hands (keep them down at your side). Suggestions for activities during break-time may help in the same way. You could suggest 'going on a bug hunt' (looking for insects in a patch of ground that is not on a main thoroughfare and which is within permitted bounds). Another possibility might be 'doing a circuit' (running a prescribed route – perhaps from one door to another via the far wall) and timing the circuit with a watch.

The loneliness of the pupil with AS becomes apparent when you observe him at break-time, although it is important that you do not interpret his solitude with non-AS eyes. Without intervention he may find it very difficult to 'play', to join in with other children with their complex games and social rules, although it may be equally true that what he needs is some space to recharge his batteries in solitude. There is much to be said for allocating support for a pupil with AS through break-time, even if it means reduced support during some lessons. After all, AS is a social deficit, and explicit, taught social rules and strategies will allow for very real learning, even if it is not academic learning. Equally, adult supervision may be required if the child with AS is to be allowed to use the time to take himself off to the quiet space (*see* section 3.2) or the library.

As a last resort, there is nothing wrong with the teacher or TA protecting the pupil with AS by giving him a job to do during this time. This may be solitary, or it may be an opportunity to support him in working with a partner. Perhaps he and another pupil might be allowed to stay in to tidy the book corner, to feed the fish or clean the whiteboards. Perhaps they could be asked to take the paper from the green bins to the recycling point. What is to say that these pupils cannot be given status ('Green Monitors', for example) so that 'break-time' becomes a structured and useful time?

Having done this, though, the teacher does need to be aware that where all the other pupils have had their 'time off' to recharge their batteries, the pupil with AS has not. If for the first ten minutes of the next lesson he needs to read, or just to go off into his inner world for a while, that is perhaps understandable and excusable. A pupil with AS will be able to look after himself and recharge in his own way if allowed space to do so. Just because he does this in a different way to the rest of the class does not mean it is any less valid. After all, the teacher has probably just spent the last quarter of an hour drinking coffee and talking about her husband/garden/holiday. How many neurotypical eight-year-olds would think that that made sense? There is a lot to be said for letting people get on with things their own way.

2.6 Agree on rules of etiquette to avoid 'rudeness'

One of the insights that a parent has, when living with a child with AS for 24 hours a day, is how often he can appear to be rude. We become adept at intervening before trouble escalates. Perhaps our child pushes into a line because he does not realize it is there. Perhaps he interrupts when someone else is talking because what he or she is saying is not relevant to what he is going to say. Perhaps he tells someone that they are wrong when their version of the facts does not tally with his own, or he instructs the youth with his feet up on the train seat that there is a notice on the window saying that this is not permitted. He may also ask questions: Why does that man have only one leg? Why does that woman have hair growing out of her nose?

We, as family, spend many long hours diffusing these situations, explaining, hushing or apologizing. When our child with AS goes into school, he does so without us there as 'interpreters'.

Initially, this is not a problem. Many five-year-olds will act in this way, and their behaviour is managed by the teacher who works with the whole group of five-year-olds on empathy, and on understanding the effect of what they say on other people. If this worked on *our children*, there would not be a problem! Unfortunately, this 'mind blindness', this inability to understand a situation from a perspective other than his own, is one of the elements of the diagnosis of a child with AS. Other children, by age seven or eight, have grasped it; the child with AS has not, and as he grows up, his social faux pas become a greater and greater problem.

As with everything, working on this has to happen across a home–school context. It is no good, if at home, we have agreed that the child says 'Excuse me' before speaking, when at school the rule is, instead, to put up his hand and wait until he is asked to speak. Rules have to be consistent, and a great deal more clearly thought out than that. Let us think about it for a moment: it might be that 'Excuse me' is the correct technique to use if two or three adults are talking, and the child wants to make a comment or a request unrelated to the topic being discussed. However, if the comment is on the same topic, then it might be the rule to wait until a pause and then to say it, without saying 'Excuse me' first. However, if a teacher only is talking – or any adult is addressing a group of people, for example in assembly – then, 'Excuse me' becomes inappropriate ('interrupting'), speaking in a pause is inappropriate ('shouting out') and putting up a hand is only possibly appropriate (right in a classroom context, wrong in assembly and wrong for the whole of life after the age of about 16). Social rules are immensely complex! This, of course, is why they are so hard to teach and why they are so confusing for the person with AS. The trouble is that getting them wrong, particularly if doing so leads to rebuke or even punishment, can make the person with AS very nervous about them. Much of the insecurity of the adult with AS comes from this 'not knowing how to behave'. How much of that anxiety, I wonder, stems from the handling of getting it wrong during school years?

Teaching the rules of social interaction and etiquette should be a huge part of the learning that takes place through the childhood of a person with AS. We could even argue that, for the child with AS, this is as important as or even more important than the formal school curriculum. A dedicated and AS-aware TA is ideally placed to work with the child on social rules in different contexts, and – as long as there is sufficient time to communicate what has been agreed – the parents can continue the same work out of school in a wider environment. This need to generalize social learning is recognized by psychologists working on AS, and it is important that the value of this work is appreciated by everyone involved with the child. It may have nothing to do with learning the difference between an adjective and an adverb, nor a square-based pyramid and a cone, but it is valuable learning nevertheless for that child.

Perhaps just as important, though, is how the various parties react when the child gets it wrong. No amount of social teaching is, after all, going to help the person with AS to get it right all the time – or even most of the time. The reaction when he gets it wrong is all-important.

Perhaps he pipes up in the middle of assembly and tells the headteacher that something she has said is inaccurate. Perhaps he calls out, 'Excuse me' in the middle of the Christmas sermon and tells the priest what gift he hopes to get this year. Perhaps he puts his hand up in the middle of the awards ceremony and distracts the visiting speaker. None of these are done with malice, but if he is told off for them, laughed at, ridiculed or even punished, how likely is it that in time the child will withdraw from social interaction just in case he gets it wrong?

If the whole school community knows your child, understands him and – best of all – *likes* him, these mistakes will be absorbed easily and he can be helped to act more appropriately without suffering damage for his mistakes. If your son is seen as 'quirky', as funny, bright, unusual and different but also as honest, well-intentioned and naively open-hearted, he is likely to survive the whole experience and emerge as a confident, happy and self-assured adult. He will be an adult with AS. If he is confident that having AS is 'OK', if he acknowledges that he will make social mistakes and is happy to be corrected, or to laugh along with the funny side of them when they are explained, then he is going to be OK in life. School, seen in this context, has a huge responsibility for his future well-being. It is so important that all parties work together to get this right.

2.7 Request differentiation to avoid problems

What can be hardest for parents, as you try to support your child in school, is that you are in effect admitting to his 'disability'. By getting so involved you are accepting that your son's AS makes him different, you are acknowledging this difference and requesting that this difference be accepted and respected by all in school. This can be quite hard to do. We may have tried to keep the diagnosis a secret. We may be unsure how much about the diagnosis to share with our child, or how much to share with other parents and children. The result can be confusion when we want our child treated differently – but we don't want our child treated differently! It is important that we resolve this conflict in our own minds, and make our decision clear to the teacher and staff before we try to support our child in school.

Much of the practical work on supporting the child with AS in the classroom comes from this acceptance of difference. If we insist that he be treated the same as every other child, or if the teacher insists on treating him as such, then it is going to be very difficult to accommodate his AS. He has Asperger syndrome. He is different from the other children. Different is not 'worse', but neither is it 'the same'.

Your child may find it difficult to sit in the middle of a group of children. The solution, once this is accepted, may be simple. You can ask that he sits at the end of the row in assembly, or that his seat is at the end of the table. It may be that he finds it hard to stand in a line. He could be the child who goes first when the class leaves the classroom, who holds the door open for everyone else and who then joins the very back of the line, leaving a little space. He may find it difficult to join in at circle time. Perhaps he could be made 'pencil monitor', and use that time to go round gathering up all the pencils from each table that need sharpening. Perhaps he does not like pushing and shoving to put on coats and outdoor shoes before winter break-time. This could be an opportunity for him to take the lunch lists along to the office, and put his gear on later when the other children have gone out. Differentiation is not difficult when you have understanding and motivated staff. Once the teacher is aware of the differences of a child with AS, she will probably be highly skilled at finding ways around them.

However, there is still the problem of what the other children think. Children are acutely aware of unfairness, and if the child with AS is being treated differently, and they are not told why, this may lead to resentment and to aggressive or non-accepting behaviour from the rest of the class towards the child with AS. It is not much use sheltering the child from his peers knowing that he is different if all that happens is that, instead, they see him as the 'Teacher's Pet'.

I favour openness with all the children, and with their parents. Asperger syndrome is nothing to be ashamed of! It is usually better to be open about the facts rather than allow misconception or rumour to take over. Talk to the class teacher about how this is best handled. Your child might be supported to give a presentation to his class about all the good things about having AS or about all the famous and successful people who have had it. One of the specialists mentioned earlier (*see* Chapter 1) might be able to come in and take a training session, both with the children and separately with staff and any parents who wanted to attend. You might decide to run a session yourself, perhaps invite questions from the class that you, your child or the teacher could answer. The class could do a project for personal and social education (PSE) on AS. You could put a display together for one of the school display boards. There are many possibilities and this will depend also on what the class teacher and the school in general feel is best or is current policy. It is, though, best to be proactive. Pretending the child with AS is the same as everyone else is a recipe for disaster. AS is like the monster under the bed: it doesn't go away just because you don't look at it!

2.8 Reproduce work to be done in a more accessible format

Often, a child with AS fails to achieve academically because it is not clear to him what work is required. He is likely to work better if he knows exactly what to do, where, how much to write, how long to take and how to know when a piece of work is finished. He may be foxed by an initial instruction and fail to get past that to the work which he can do. The use of spoken language and instructions (*see* Section 2.12) is important here, but so is the way work is presented visually.

Some children with AS find it easiest to write an answer in a printed a box. This gives them a clear indication of where to write, and to an extent how much to write (especially if the size of box is considered carefully, taking into account the child's individual writing style). A child with AS may also find it less distracting if only one question plus an answer box appears on each page. It may seem wasteful of paper, but it is not impossible to reproduce work as set for the rest of the class in a more visually accessible style in this way. If as a parent you volunteer to do this for, say, a test, you have a chance to see if it helps. If it does, it is not unreasonable to ask the school to produce work for your son in this format, but it is useful to prove it is effective before expecting the staff to do the extra work. It is important also to be clear what the purpose of a piece of work is. If, for example, it is to show the sequence of events in a book, this could perhaps be done by drawing stick-figure representations of the major events, and then encouraging the child with AS to cut and paste them into order. The parts of a plant could be identified by filling in labels. History facts could be tested by asking the child to cross out untrue or unsubstantiated facts. Often it will take a bit of imagination to find ways of allowing a pupil with AS to show his understanding in the clearest light, but it is well worth the effort. A TA who has worked successfully with your child in previous years may be the best person to go to for advice about what has worked before, and to build on this technique.

It may also pay to work with the child on strategies to do with leaving work that he cannot do and moving on. One symptom of AS may be that the child finds it extremely difficult to 'give up' on something and move on to something else. Faced with ten questions, he may get stuck on the first and get no further. It may be that his teachers and support staff need to come up with specific ways around this. For example, it might be agreed that after a certain length of time struggling on one question, your child should mark that question with a star and go on to the next one, returning to the starred ones at the end only if he has time. With a strategy such as this it is important (as usual!) to communicate the technique to other teachers and to you, so that the child can be supported to use it over different subject areas and at home for homework. He will also need to be supported as to occasions when *not* to use it (which may, sadly, be often).

2.9 Provide a laptop

The child with AS being educated in the twenty-first century is luckier than his predecessors. Not only does he have his condition recognized, but he also has computers to help him. Many of the visually presented suggestions made in the last section are strategies that work well on a computer. Fill-the-blanks, cut-and-paste, moving texts or pictures around to categorize them into different groups, multichoice answers – all are techniques that are easy to manage on a computer. Many children with AS struggle with handwriting. There is much to be said for supporting them in learning to touch-type, and indeed for helping them with word-prediction software and even voice-recognition software to help them to overcome this disadvantage. Yes, writing is useful, but the way we use writing is changing. Few people write now for anyone but themselves to read (you may write a shopping list or scribble yourself a reminder note, but if you are going to write to the bank manager, you type. You probably use email anyway!) Even grammar rules are fluid, as speed communication – texting and the like – become the norm. In this context schools are behind the times when they spend so long teaching neat, cursive handwriting. What is essential is that your child is supported to communicate. A laptop computer of his own is likely to be the most useful tool for him to have.

One day in the not too distant future it is likely that each child will have his or her own laptop at school. In the meantime, few schools have enough computers in the classrooms for more than one or two children to use them at a time. It is a relatively simple solution to bypass this problem by supplying your child with AS with a laptop of his own. There are even laptops on the market designed for use in school, although this is not strictly necessary. He will not need anything too sophisticated for this. An old, recon-

ditioned machine is likely to be fine, as is a more simple 'word pro-
cessor' type of machine.

With a laptop, and with some technical support available to
help him use it, it may be possible for your child to interface with
the classroom interactive whiteboard. He may be able to download
work, put together presentations and share his work with the class.
He can work in any place, using the same material as the other
children but in a different medium. Thus he can retire to a quiet
space (*see* section 3.2) and get on away from distractions, may work
at a workstation or sit at the table with his peers. Proficiency with a
laptop computer is a skill to carry with him into secondary school
and into adult life. The sooner he can be supported in using one,
the better.

2.10 Discuss provision of a workstation

The concept of a workstation is something that has emerged from
the work of Division TEACCH (Treatment and Education of
Autistic and Related Communication-handicapped CHildren) from
the Univeristy of North Carolina, USA. The concept of TEACCH is
large, but one aspect of it, the workstation, is fairly easy to extract.
The idea is that the pupil is given a space of his own, somewhere
that is distraction-free and not visually overstimulating. In this
space the pupil works always to the principle of top to bottom, left
to right. He might have a series of drawers or trays on his left, in
which is placed one piece of work per tray, including everything
needed to complete that work. He starts on the left, at the top, takes
his instructions and equipment for that piece of work out of the
tray and completes the work. When it is finished (and what constitutes 'finished' is made very clear in the instructions), he places
everything in a 'Finished' tray to his right. He then turns to the
next tray down on the left, removes the items, does the work and

places it in the finished tray on the right, and so on. Using this technique, the child can work independently on a number of pieces of work, their contents varying depending on the subjects being studied. The technique helps the teacher to focus on what, precisely, is required for that piece of work, how to issue that instruction visually and what materials are needed. It may be that a pencil and eraser need to appear in trays one, two and four. In this case, the pupil will need three pencils and three erasers. Although this may seem unnecessary to most neurotypical people, it is not hard to see how many hours of schooling are lost to the pupil with AS because he does not have a pencil, does not know where to write, does not know what is required of him. The beauty of a workstation is that it makes focussing on what is required the priority for both pupil and teacher, and it allows independent working. The bottom tray on the left should contain something which the pupil enjoys doing – perhaps a book around his special interest, a construction set or a computer game. He knows that when he has finished the work in each of the trays he will arrive at this one and this motivates him to keep going.

The workstation technique seems to work well, often with students with fairly 'low functioning' autism. It may seem a little sterile to the neurotypical person, but its orderliness and predictability seem to appeal to many people with conditions on the autistic spectrum, and it may well be something that is worth trying in the classroom with a pupil with AS. Certainly the child with AS may find it very hard to 'get down to work' when seated at a table with a number of other pupils, all of whom may be moving, muttering or mumbling, and whose books, belongings or elbows may at any time invade his own sense of space. Although I would not suggest that the pupil with AS be confined to a workstation for too much of the day, it might well provide the still haven in the classroom for periods of quiet work which he craves. If it is also the place where he keeps his laptop computer, and therefore becomes the place where he can tune out the rest of the class and get on in his own way, it may well be a great asset, and is certainly worth trying.

2.11 Build a quiet area in class

As discussed in more detail in Chapter 3, your child may benefit from having access to a sanctuary. It may be that he needs some-where where he can 'get away' from other people, from an over-stimulating environment, from noises, lights, smells and from social demands.

Quite often a young pupil with AS will decide on his own 'safe haven', quite often under a table or behind the curtains. Although it is important to respect his need to go to this place, it is likely to work better if you can agree a place that is more socially acceptable. It takes a confident teacher to allow a child to sit under the table for any length of time without feeling that she should do something about it, and the other children are going to see his behaviour as 'odd'.

It is better if the teacher and your child can decide on a place where he can go when he needs some 'space', and agree when it is appropriate for him to use it. You might agree, for example, on the book corner, which in many classrooms already has an element of screening around it and perhaps some cushions or beanbags to sit on. Work with your child and with the class teacher on ways of making the space attractive to him. You could bring in books from home that you know he likes, or a favourite cushion or rug from home that you know he likes to lie on (or under!). It may be possible to supply some music for him to listen to on headphones, or even a small toy or puzzle. See section 3.2 for more details about the use of quiet areas, and about the provision of a quiet space in school.

2.12 Work with the teacher on the use of language

One area where you can help your child's class teacher is to talk to her about her use of language. She may be becoming frustrated because your son seems to be ignoring her, or refusing to do as he is asked. Getting her to think about how she words requests may be a big help, and agree with her some simple strategies.

One of the easiest is the strategy of 'name before instruction'. It may be that the child with AS is appearing to ignore the teacher because he literally does not realize that she is talking to him. He is probably filtering out what she says as irrelevant to him, and is confused, then, when she wants him to do something and he does not know what it is. A general rule with children with AS is to speak less, and allow processing time before expecting an answer. If your child's teacher wants him to do something, she would be well-advised to say his name first, wait until his attention has shifted from what he was doing to her, and then make the request clearly in simple, non-figurative language. If the teacher wants the child to answer a question, again, say his name first, ask the question and allow time for him to sort out the words for the answer. Repeating the question, particularly in a different format, will not help. Indeed, where it is common to clarify when a neurotypical child is struggling to answer and to change the wording of the question or 'put it another way', for a child with AS this may be simply confusing. He has to wait for you to stop, decide which question you want answering and then go back to trying to sort out that answer into words. Keeping questions short and unambiguous, and allowing plenty of time to process the answer can make a huge difference.

A child with AS may become distracted by apparent inconsistencies in what is said. One five-year-old I observed became distressed during a lesson on direction and the use of left and right, because his teacher was describing the route from school to her *house* – and he knew she lived in a *bungalow.* If problems occur in class, it is always good to get the teacher to think back over what she actually said, as opposed to what she meant. Often, the reason for the problem may be found there, and with a little practice the teacher can become adept at spotting the problems before they get out of hand.

2.13 Ask that the learning goals of each session be made explicit, preferably in visual form

Schools have become much better at sharing the learning objectives of the lesson with the pupils, yet much learning in school is still inferred. Often, children do not realize what they are learning. As far as they are concerned they are listening to a story or playing a game, but really there is a hidden learning goal. This works brilliantly for the neurotypical child, who soon makes the connections and is able to generalize understanding across different contexts.

It does not work so well for the child with AS. If he does not know that he knows something, he may lack the ability to access that knowledge. He may be able to recite what the class agreed about how many lions there were in the pride after each of the four lionesses gave birth to four cubs, but he does not know that he can work out '4×4'.

It is important that what the child has learnt is made very clear to him, and that it is recorded for him to refer back to. At the end of the lesson on lions, it is important that the child works out some simple numerical arithmetic sums, and it should be made clear to him that the technique for this is the same if he is calculating lions, bananas or the money in his pocket. It is important to record for the child that he can work out multiplication facts around the 'four times table'. He will then be more likely to be able to access that knowledge again next time he needs it.

If using a workstation, this is the ideal place for this knowledge to be reinforced. The lesson may have been about lions, but the work presented in the workstation could be about four times tables. In addition, over the course of the week there may be additional problems set for the pupil, about lions, apples, leaves on a tree and sandwiches in a lunch box. Generalization of knowledge, and the ability to apply the same techniques over different contexts, are aspects of learning which are likely to require considerably more attention from the pupil with AS than his neurotypical peers.

2.14 Encourage peer support

Some of the best support for a child with AS may come from the other children in his class. Children will often help each other, but if the teacher has said that there is to be no talking, the child with AS is unlikely to accept any help. If the official rule of the classroom is 'No Copying', he will not be able to glance at the work done by the child beside him and be reassured that his work looks the same. If he is to access support from his peers, this will have to be facilitated by the teacher.

You can ask the teacher to come up with some strategies for this. Perhaps she can pair him to work at a task with one particular child. Perhaps she can say, specifically, that if he gets stuck it is OK to look across and see what the pupil next to him is doing, or to ask his neighbour for help. Encouraging the rest of the class to see that helping the child with AS is a positive thing can make a big difference to how much he is accepted socially. If his peers know that they will always be credited if they help him, if they know to look out for him and to be aware that he might sometimes get instructions muddled up, and if they are confident that they will not be in trouble if they are working with him, this will all lead to a more inclusive environment. Some schools operate a system where older pupils visit the classrooms of the younger ones and work with them. Even if this is not routine policy at your child's school, you could request it, especially if there is an older child with AS already in the school. It is likely to improve self-esteem all round if this child is encouraged to come and work with your child sometimes and if your child is then encouraged to work with a younger pupil later on. Nor need this help always suggest that it is the child with AS who is the weaker. If he has a particular strength – perhaps an aptitude for science, computers, music or art – your child could be encouraged to help others if they are stuck, and his peers should be made aware that this is allowed and that they may turn to him for assistance. Peer support, if it can be managed, is likely to be the most useful support for the child with AS in the long term. Adult support is inherently limited and will, anyway, not always be there. If the child with AS can get to a point where he knows it is OK to turn to those around him to support him when he is in difficulty, many of his problems will be solved.

2.15 Value the work done by the class teacher and the TA

You are asking a great deal of your child's teacher or TA. This is fair enough – your child deserves the best education that, between you, you can achieve. It is not a bad idea, though, to make sure that the quality of this work is recognized by all involved. Credit the dedication of the members of staff working with your child by making sure that the school is aware of it. Letters of praise or thanks to them, copied to the headteacher can do no harm. Nor need it stop there. With their (and the school's) permission you could go further in crediting the work the staff do to your local community. You could write an article commending the good practice at work in your child's class for the local newspaper, or for magazines. Often,

Asperger publications or websites invite people to give examples of what is working for people with AS. You could include in these all the good things achieved by your child's school, and ensure that credit is given. All too often the only time individual members of staff or schools come to public attention are because of what they do not do, or because of what they are doing badly. Taking the time to articulate all the good work that is going on in your child's school will both allow staff to be acknowledged for their excellence, and make it more likely that this good practice will be repeated. By raising the profile of those who are working to 'make school make sense' to pupils with AS, you will be raising their status and making what they are doing more valued.

3

Whole-school Solutions

Ultimately, the success or otherwise of your child with AS at school will be a matter of whole-school policy. Just as there is a limit to the support you may give him without the co-operation and encouragement of his teacher and support staff, so their ability to help him may be hindered if they do not have the understanding of the school authorities. Much of what they are required to do in the classroom will have been determined by the headteacher, and an individual teacher may not have the authority to alter that herself. If you want the environment of the school to be genuinely Asperger-appropriate, you may have to tackle the issue yourself.

Unfortunately, it is at this level, at the level of the headteacher, that you are least likely to come across AS-specific training. To have risen to headteacher position, most teachers will have been in the profession for some years, and it is unlikely that there was any information about AS available when they trained. Headteachers have a difficult, demanding and time-consuming job. They have to balance the needs of all pupils and all members of staff with more abstract concerns such as educational philosophies and learning initiatives. They have to keep up to date with new legislation, with government demands and with local and regional as well as national initiatives. It may be that they will have had neither time nor opportunity to become more than superficially acquainted with the specific needs of pupils with AS.

On the other hand, most headteachers have risen to their position because they are good at their job and because they care deeply about the welfare of the pupils in their care. It is likely that their lack of Asperger understanding may be attributed to circumstances, not lack of interest. If you can make suggestions that make sense, do not cost too much money or demand too much in terms of time or resources, and which may, in fact, benefit all the pupils in the school, there is every chance these will be most welcome. It is natural to feel slightly intimidated by headteachers. They carry an aura of authority left over from our own awe of our headteacher when we were at school. In addition, we are likely to be aware of how phenomenally busy they are, and be tentative about demanding their time. We should overcome this timidity, be clear about what we are requesting and devise solutions as well as raising problems. We have Asperger understanding, and we understand our child's specific needs. If we can share that knowledge with the school, we are an asset and should have the confidence that we will be seen as such.

3.1 Request explicit rules

One of the first things to discuss with the headteacher is the notion that your child cannot be understood to break a rule unless this rule is made clear. This concept may be more complicated than it at first appears. Many schools have dispensed with school rules (which sound old-fashioned and draconian) and instead have things like 'Codes of Conduct', listing expectations such as 'Pupils are expected to act with courtesy towards members of staff and each other'. These non-specifics are little help for the child with AS.

You may need to discuss with the headteacher exactly what the rules (and expectations) of the school are, for they will be there, even if they are largely implied. For example, pupils might be required to address adults by name. They might be expected to walk (not run) in the corridors. They might be expected to keep left on the stairs. They might be expected to ask for permission to leave class to go to the bathroom. These are all fairly simple. However, less obvious to the pupil with AS, they may be expected to keep their shoes (and clothes) on in the classroom, to leave display boards alone (and not take out all the pins), not to hug their teacher if pleased to see her, not to walk into the staff room. They may be expected to leave electric sockets alone and not to unplug the school computer system, or – even more importantly – they may be expected to stay on the school site and not try to walk home. These rules, inferred by the majority of pupils, should be made explicit to the pupil with AS if they are to be obeyed. More importantly, if they are 'broken' the child with AS must not be in trouble until staff are sure that he understood that the rule was there.

Perhaps the best people to come up with a list of 'real' school rules are the older pupils. Pupils in the top years of the school could find it an interesting exercise, and, since they are more likely to be aware of the child's perspective, are more likely to know what to include. If there is an older pupil with a diagnosis of AS already in the school, this might be a good commission for him. He may have had to elicit these rules for himself by trial and error, and is likely to be ideally placed to articulate them for the younger pupil with AS.

Clearly, no one could come up with a full list covering every single aspect of school life (and if they did, it would be far too long for the child with AS to take in). However, if the child with AS appears to be getting into trouble in an area of the school, looking at the rules that govern that area may be well worthwhile. Sometimes it may be as simple as a child with AS who 'takes things' being unsure about which items in school are shared and which are personal to individuals. Clarifying that the pencils in the tray on the table are for everyone, but those in another child's pencil case are not, may be a good place to start.

It is a good place to start because, until rules are explicit, your child should not be in trouble if he breaks them. If your relationship with the headteacher, and with the school, is to be a good one, it is important that your child does not start off by being in trouble. Requesting clear rules both helps him to abide by them, and begins to explain to the headteacher the problems that he faces. What is needed, perhaps more than anything else, is Asperger understanding, a way of thinking that allows those in authority at the school to see things from an Asperger perspective. Asking for a list of rules around a potential problem area is a good start to achieving this.

3.2 Create a quiet space

One of the most effective supports for the child with AS in school is the creation of a quiet space, a safe haven where he can retire, recharge and get himself ready to face the next peculiarity of the neurotypical world. Without this sanctuary there is the very real danger that a child with AS will run into difficulty. He may either run out of school (with all the repercussions that entails), have to create his own safe place, which may well be inappropriate or unsafe, or become overwhelmed by the sensory and social demands being made on him, and find lashing out to be the only solution.

The first response of most schools to the idea of a quiet space may well be that they have no spare space available. Members of staff who have nowhere quiet to prepare lessons or mark work may find the suggestion that an area be created to meet the needs of one pupil laughable, or even insulting. There may be a knee-jerk reaction of 'Wouldn't we all like a space of our own?' It may take some persuasion before they understand that this haven is a *need*, not a luxury, for the child with AS, and that, actually, the space could work for them as well.

The idea of a quiet space is that it is somewhere where the child with AS may go, either at his own request or at the suggestion of staff. If he starts to show signs of being overwhelmed – becoming distressed and withdrawn or becoming louder and 'aggressive' – the quiet space is an option for him to calm down and regain control of his environment. This space should, fairly obviously, be a place of quiet and minimal stimulation, somewhere away from the movement of children around the school, from the smells of the dining hall and the noise of the music room, somewhere that does not have electronic equipment but which is plain, still and calm. The child with AS could keep a bag, tray or locker there with some of his things, perhaps books or items around his special interest, and could be given time to use his own techniques to relax and 'regroup'.

It is important that the space is staffed, or at least in a place where adults are passing or which adults are aware of. Somewhere too isolated may lead to abuse of the facility, or to the potential for bullying.

Of course it need not be a room. The above description may well already fit the reception area of the school or the area outside the headteacher's office. It may be that the library or book area fits the description, too, or the secretary's office, the medical room or even the staff planning and preparation area. Schools may have to be innovative in finding the space, but once the staff are aware of the benefits it offers, they should find it well worth the effort.

The quiet space works best if the child has an always respected, 'get out of jail free' card which means that he can *always* access it. This card may be, literally, a card – perhaps a laminated token that he can present when words fail him and which allows him to escape at once, without question, to his haven. Of course, whatever the child was doing at the time (or not doing!) still has to be faced up to and resolved, but the card offers an alternative to being overwhelmed, to lashing out, breaking down or finding himself in far bigger trouble.

It is important that the quiet space is never used for punishment. Nor is access to it used as a motivator for the child. It must be seen as purely therapeutic, a necessary remedy to the non-AS suitability of the rest of the environment. It is respectful of the child's autism. It is, if you like, an acknowledgement that school cannot help but be a stressful place for someone with AS. It carries with it an expectation that the child conforms to the neurotypical expectations demanded of him, but it is also an apology, a concession that at least one place be provided which is appropriate to his needs.

It may also be an attractive asset to the school, to other pupils and to staff. The area chosen might be most effective if dotted with plants, supplemented by comfortable chairs, perhaps enhanced by a tropical fish-tank. How much more likely is it that funding be found for such things if they are seen as essential special educational needs provision, and not inessential window-dressing? The school may yet find your child with AS a tremendous asset.

3.3 Create break-time zones

As discussed in Chapter 2, break-time may be very difficult for a child with AS. The schoolyard may seem to him an utterly alien environment. It may seem like a vast, featureless space in which children (none of whom he may even recognize) charge around making lots of noise, changing direction apparently randomly and engaging in meaningless, even aggressive-seeming behaviour.

Being made to go into this environment is hardly going to be a 'break' for the child with AS, which 'break-time' is designed to be.

Yet children with AS need a break from lessons just as everyone else does. They, too, benefit from fresh air, exercise and a chance to let off steam. Yes, if the school's outside play area cannot be made into a safe or attractive environment for them, the option to stay indoors in a quieter place is a good compromise. However, there are ways that the schoolyard can be made acceptable, but they require willingness and imagination as much as money. If you are willing to get together with a group of parents over a weekend and put in some of the physical work, there is no reason why the play area cannot be transformed and improved, for all the children, not just your child with AS.

The easiest ways to 'break up' the featureless wastes of the outside play area are to provide visual supports. A line around the edge of the ball area may be a tremendous help in clarifying just where that area is. A painted line on the ground can make a path from one building to the next, or a 'safe path' to a quiet area. A quiet area may be simply a couple of benches in the corner of the yard, perhaps with a tub or two of flowers partially screening them from the rest. Again, a painted line around the area helps make it clear where its limits are, and a sign made by the children could clarify the areas rules: that it is an area for sitting quietly, chatting or reading.

For more energetic play, painting symbols on the floor can make for all sorts of games, most of which have clear and understandable rules for the child with AS. These may be anything from hopscotch to stepping stones, from a painted 'road' to balance lines and number lines, from 'islands' to targets to be aimed at with a beanbag. Appointing and training 'break-time buddies' from the older classes can work well, as they can help set up more formal games and arbitrate disputes. Again, some sort of visual clue may help to identify them, whether it be a coloured cap, a sash or a T-shirt.

Another great idea is to have a zone – again, visually identifiable – where there is a 'craze of the week'. Again, this is set up and managed by members of staff or the break-time buddies, and might be anything from coin spinning, long rope skipping or card swapping to cat's cradle, and changing on a weekly basis. The point is that it gives the child with AS (and any other child finding socializing during this otherwise unstructured time a problem) something to do – something which has rules, a place, may be understood and which is supervised.

Most of these ideas are good ones for all children, but as usual the organizer needs to see things a little differently if she is going to adapt the idea of break-time zones to benefit the child with AS. Many schools have a 'buddy stop', a place to go if you have no one to play with, and from where allocated break-time buddies collect you and take you off. This can be brilliant for including the shy child or even the socially isolated child, but it may be the very last thing a child with AS needs. Care should be taken not to force a child with AS to be sociable, especially during a period of the day designated as being a time which is supposed to recharge the batteries. Much can be done, as suggested, to make it easier for a child with AS to join in if he wants to. However, if he does not, then that should be respected, too. Many children with AS spend their break-times going around the edges of the play area. It may be that this is the clearest 'area' that they can find, or it may be that this is the quietest part of the yard. They may benefit from an allocated area that does not try to be sociable. Perhaps a 'wildlife zone' could be created – an otherwise scruffy corner of the outside play area where no running is allowed, and where everyone is encouraged to tread carefully and speak as little as possible so as not to disturb the various bugs and worms. Alternatively, the child could be encouraged to use the quiet area and to take a book or a favourite toy there.

All of these provisions can make for a happier play area for children with AS, but a note of caution: it is imperative that these zones are staffed and that they do not become areas where the isolated child may become more vulnerable to bullying. A quiet area needs to be somewhere where members of staff go routinely to eat their sandwiches or have a drink. A wildlife zone needs to be visited throughout break-time by duty staff, and perhaps even have a 'warden' appointed to keep an eye on it. A pupil with AS is arguably more vulnerable during break-time than during any other part of the school day. It is a time to give support, and it is not unreasonable as a parent to request support at this time, even if it means reduced support in the comparative 'safety' of the classroom.

3.4 Draw together shared expertise and work on transitions

One of the most worrying aspects of observing a child with AS at school, is just how quickly and how badly things can go wrong. A child may be 'fine' throughout his school career until one particular point, and then within a matter of a couple of days become self-violent, swear, assault a teacher or another pupil, destroy property or run out of school. At this point, none of the school's usual approaches or sanctions are seen to work, and despair sets in very quickly. From a parent's point of view all this can be overwhelming. We are left saying, 'But I thought he was doing so well...' The sad thing is that he probably was.

This sort of crisis is most likely to have occurred because of lack of understanding of AS by otherwise dedicated, professional and well-meaning members of staff. AS can be very hard to get your head around. The pupil with AS may seem to be very little different from any other pupil. He may not fit any of the staff's preconceived notions of 'autistic', and they may even start to question the diagnosis. Initial caution may fade away, and gradually the need for support may be questioned. If the child does not display any signs of distress, is not disruptive or difficult, is not noticeably withdrawn or isolated, is managing to cope to a reasonable academic level then it may be believed that there isn't an issue. His AS is forgotten.

Yet the child has not stopped having AS. He may not be showing many 'symptoms', but the underlying difference is still there. The way he perceives the world remains fundamentally different. It only takes a member of staff to forget this, or not to appreciate this, for devastation to set in.

To give an example: When asked to make a change to a piece of work, Alan, an eight-year-old with AS instead told his new teacher, 'This is a warning' and gave her a piece of paper on which he had written: 'CAREFUL!' Fortunately, the teacher in question happened to be highly aware of AS. She did not respond, as many teachers would, to the apparent inappropriateness of this. Even though it may be hard see this as appropriate behaviour for an eight-year-old, she was able to understand it as such. From Alan's point of view, he was with a new teacher. Although he appeared to be managing well, this was putting considerable hidden strain on him. With his previous teacher he had been working on using visual cues, and on communicating when he was having difficulty. The teacher had been using written 'stories' to explain what was happening, and had been trying to get Alan to indicate when he was starting to get anxious or angry, before the feelings overwhelmed him. In this context, it becomes apparent that Alan's letter was entirely appropriate. He used the same technique as had been used with him – a written 'story'– and used it to indicate that some aspect of what was happening was getting too much for him.

Had he been more articulate, and had been able to write, 'I am aware that I am beginning to experience sensory overload. I am concerned that if you do not allow me to conclude this activity and take myself off into the book corner for some time alone to steady myself, my behaviour may become erratic', no one would have questioned his appropriateness. For Alan at eight, already under pressure, a written 'CAREFUL!' was not a bad effort!

In Alan's case this was recognized by his teacher, who was already working closely with his previous teacher on the transition. Because of their joint understanding, Alan's behaviour was accepted and even celebrated. Yet, if this had not been the case, and if the new teacher had responded simply to the impression given by the note, the result can be imagined all too clearly. Alan was already indicating high stress levels. He is unlikely to have coped if his survival strategy had been ignored and even ridiculed. If he had been reprimanded for the 'inappropriate' note, the result was likely to have been catastrophic. If his use of techniques that had been recommended to him had failed, he might not only have lost control of that particular situation, but have lost confidence that the strategies work. If he were then further punished for the inevitable outbreak, the spiral down would be almost certain.

What is needed as the child moves up through the school is time (that ever-scarce resource!) for the teacher or teaching assistant (TA), or both, who have worked with your child in one year to pass on information to his new teacher and support staff. Ideally, the TA at least should be able to come into the classroom and observe the teacher and child in their old context before the change of year. There needs to be confidence between teachers that what is happening is not an implied criticism of the new teacher's expertise, but merely awareness that after a year or more together, the previous teacher will have a bank of experience of your child with AS to draw on. Nor should that experience be lost after your child has moved on. What is needed when things go wrong is a kind of 'rapid response team', which knows the child and may shed light on the reasons behind what is happening. There should be a pool of understanding of the child which has grown throughout his time at that school. The team might include the current and previous teachers, TAs past and present, the special education team and, of course, the parents. It might also include the child himself. As long as there is the basic premise that the behaviour had a reason (and was neither 'naughty' nor attention-seeking), this group have a good chance of playing detective and working out what went wrong. This is far more important than reacting to what the child did. Yes, he may have put his fist through the window – but *why?* (*see* section 3.5).

3.5 Request a pupil 'incident log'

One of the recurring and oft-repeated themes of this book is the need for communication. It is such a major theme both because it is so important and because it is so difficult to achieve in schools. Staff have very little time in the ordinary day when they can talk to each other. Where adults in an office context, for example, may have many opportunities in which to discuss matters relating to their work with others, in schools the day moves relentlessly on. Most of this day is spent getting on with meeting the needs of 30 or so children at a time (usually, as the only adult meeting those needs) and teachers may simply not have the opportunity to pick over the complex reasons behind the often-confusing behaviours of one member of the class. What your child with AS does may often not make sense unless very carefully analysed by someone with an AS-perceptive eye and with the time to observe carefully over an extended period of time. That person may simply not exist in school.

As a parent you have the understanding of AS and of your own child, and are therefore in a position to be able to make this analysis. However, to do so you need to know what is going on, and the context. As mentioned earlier, you may all agree that your child has put his fist through the window. The challenge is to work out why. There will be many more much smaller and less dramatic incidents than this, and understanding them can be a major component in helping your child to achieve at school and to avoid trouble before it happens.

A good start in achieving this is to persuade the school as a whole to keep a pupil incidents log. This can be very simple – just a record of behaviour that is unusual or concerning, recorded by whoever witnessed it whether teacher, TA, lunchtime supervisor or whoever, set out in a formal way. The log needs to have a column that describes the behaviour (not the effect of the behaviour – so it would read 'He hit the window' not 'He broke the window'), and which records what happened before the incident, and the immediate effect of the incident. This is designed to prevent leaping to conclusions when the action is seen from a neurotypical point of view.

It may be that the incident appears to be that your child smashed a window in fury because he was not allowed to play football. It may be, when the incident is analysed, that that is not what happened at all. Perhaps immediately preceding the incident, your child had tried to take the football away from a group of players, and they had objected and taken it back. Your child then smashed a window. Conclusion: he had a fit of temper because of his inability to articulate his anger at not being allowed to play.

However, if you go back a little further, the previous lesson was science, where the properties of glass were discussed, and the fact that glass is a liquid was explained. This fascinated your son, who wanted to use the ball to throw against the window to see if the glass would react like throwing a stone into a pond. When he could not get the ball away from the players, and realizing that break-time was nearly over, he used his hand instead, to see whether his fist could push into the liquid of the glass. It couldn't. The window broke because glass does not react in the same way as other liquids, not because it was smashed in fury.

The way this incident should be dealt with must reflect the incident itself. Once the motivation behind the episode is understood, some work could be done constructively on conducting safe experiments, or on talking experiments through with an adult before they are carried out. Of course, your son must learn that the consequence of his action was that a window was broken. Perhaps he might donate his pocket money for the next few weeks to pay for its replacement. After all, he did not conduct his experiment correctly, so he should be able to understand that it is his responsibility to make good. However, what is not appropriate is that he be made to apologize for losing his temper (he didn't), nor that he be given support to join the football match. (He didn't want to join it in the first place.) If we are to help school 'make sense' to the child with AS, we have to first make sense of his world. A log is a good start in this process.

Another advantage of a pupil incident log is that it builds up a picture over a period of time. It may be that, on analysis, it is found that incidents tend to occur on a Thursday afternoon, when the violin teacher is in school, with a resulting assault to delicate hearing, or that incidents occur more in a particular room, or with a particular teacher. A log is a factual, unweighted document which should help the person 'playing detective', whoever that is, to get to the bottom of behaviours. It is important that everyone writing the log knows from the start that it may be read by parents, other teachers, TAs and perhaps even by outside professionals. It is not fair to expect what staff think of as being a private log to be thrown open without warning. We all of us (those without AS) modify our style and what we write depending on who is going to read it. It is important that openness and a non-blame culture is cultivated from the start.

3.6 Bells!

One of the very easiest ways a whole-school policy may help a child with AS is in consideration of the use of bells. Not all children with AS are sensitive to loud noises, but some are, and for them the bell, and indeed anticipation of the bell, may be so uncomfortable that all other learning is blocked. The fear that the bell will ring is ever present, so that the problem is there throughout the day, not just for the few minutes each day when the bell actually rings.

The simplest solution, although not one that every school would consider, is to stop using the bell. The bell might be used to announce the start of the school day, to indicate change of lesson, the beginning or end of break-time, or the end of the school day. If there is a clock in every classroom, surely this isn't really needed. Many schools have stopped using bells already, merely because they are outdated, intrusive and imply that school is a factory-like environment which runs to the clock and not to individuals. There are many arguments for getting rid of bells. The fact that they cause intolerable stress to even one pupil is definitely one of them.

If as a parent you really cannot persuade the school to dispense with bells, you can help relieve some of the stress by allowing your child with AS an 'early warning system'. This is a more acceptable type of alarm – a quiet beep or a silent alarm set to vibrate – which warns that the bell will ring in two minutes' time. This allows the child to prepare, to cover his ears or to move away, and it stops both the shock of the bell going off unexpectedly and the constant fearful anticipation that it will go off.

If your child is based in one classroom, you may be able to persuade the class teacher to muffle the bell in that room. It is important to be sensitive to the movements around the school of the child with AS, though, as other bells will still distress him.

The 'turn the bell off' solution really is the best one, and you could remind schools that they are expected to make 'reasonable adjustments' to make the environment inclusive for children with disabilities. This is such an easy adjustment to make. Most schools, faced with the complexities and challenges of meeting the varying needs of children with AS in their community, should welcome such a simple, instant and inexpensive option with open arms.

Incidentally, the other use of the bell is often to indicate the need to evacuate the building, usually because of fire. Clearly this is needed and serves a genuine purpose. However, most pupils experience the fire alarm only during the routine, once-a-term practices. Although it may not be ideal to warn the pupil with AS that there is going to be a fire practice, with some sensitivity it should be possible to ensure that he is away from the immediate ringing at the time it goes off, or to ensure that support staff are nearby to assist him. If the class teacher is aware that a fire practice is imminent, she may well be able to take the opportunity to send the pupil with AS, and perhaps another pupil, on a 'job' for her, perhaps to the front office, or to another classroom where the bell is fainter. Clearly, the pupil with AS will have to learn to respond appropriately to the alarm, just as everyone else does, in case there really is a fire one day. On the other hand, the school needs to be sensitive to the levels of anxiety of a pupil with AS. The reasons for fire drills, the mechanics of them and the fact that they are to protect everyone's safety may well need reinforcing.

3.7 Create occupational therapy sessions before or during school

Another provision that is relatively easy to implement is an occupational therapy session, perhaps at the beginning of each day. This sounds more of a challenge than it really is. It may be possible to persuade a member of staff to give it a try (if your child has support you might ask for this time as some of the TA's allocated hours), and to get some parents to volunteer to come in to help out.

Many children with AS have sensory integration difficulties. This means that they may be over- or undersensitive to sensory input, which may result in sensory avoidance or sensory-seeking behaviour. For example, the child may have trouble orientating himself in space. He may not be getting sufficient feedback from bones and muscles to his brain to be aware of whether he is standing, sitting, kneeling, or which way is up and which down. The result, seen in behaviour, is that he may move constantly, may balance his chair, may stand to write or, more intrusively, may bang his head against the wall, slap his face or bite himself. The most useful analogy I have heard is the way, when we have a numbing injection at the dentist, we find ourselves probing the affected area constantly with our tongue, or patting at our face with fingers, trying to get some feedback from the area to our brain. The child who is sensory-seeking will be displaying similar behaviours constantly. Similarly, a child who is sensory-avoiding may shut his eyes, cover his ears or be unable to sit in a group with other children. These are real, physical sensations for the child with AS, and awareness of them gives some insight into yet another reason why these children may not thrive at school.

An occupational therapy session at the beginning of the day could combine sensory-alerting and sensory-calming activities, to help the child to focus and bring his sensory system under control. A circuit might include some balancing – both *of* the body, on a rocker board for example, and *on* the body, for example walking with a beanbag on the head or on either shoulder. It might include activities such as bouncing on a trampoline, crawling on all fours, rolling down a slope, being rolled up in a mat or being squashed under a gym ball. A session of training from an occupational therapist with an interest in this area would be all that was needed to give members of staff and parent volunteers sufficient to get started, and the same occupational therapist could perhaps revisit after a term to see how the sessions are working. The benefit of these sessions on children with AS, and on many other children, can be substantial. They are well worth trying.

3.8 Look at identification or directions around school

Depending on the size of the building (and on the child with AS himself), it is quite possible that he may get lost in school. Partly this is because expectations are not made clear. When walking as a class in a line (or 'crocodile' – how confusing is that term to a child with AS?), it is often not said specifically that each child should follow the one in front. I have known children with AS to wander out of the line and get lost between leaving the classroom and, for example, not arriving at the hall. It may also be the case that it is not made clear to the pupil where things are. 'The Office' may refer to the secretary's office, not the head's office, and may be used synonymously with the reception desk, which is different from the reception classroom! Is Mrs C's room the room where Mrs C usually is, or where she is now? Does 'Stand in the corridor' mean stand outside the classroom or at some other point in its length? Does 'Wait outside' mean wait outside the door or outside the building? Who is to guess that 'Give this to Mr M' means put it on his desk if he is not in his room, not find out that he has taken Class 5C swimming and set off into town to the swimming pool?

As a school, there is much that can be done to help with this sort of organizational confusion. Numbering or naming rooms is far less confusing than letting rooms be known by their main teacher, especially as this is likely to change year by year. So is providing a map which can be taken home and the layout of the building explored with parents. Having a sign identifying a room on its door makes things even clearer. If the school has different sections (perhaps the children aged up to seven are taught in one part of the school, and those aged over seven in another), having the corridors painted different colours may be a huge help. Having a few well-appointed signs with arrows can make a difference too.

What is essential is that the child with AS knows of at least one place where he can go if lost or confused. This could be the front desk, staff room or the quiet space. He needs to be confident that he can get to this place from anywhere in the school. Some work can be done on this at the start of each year as his 'home base' in the school changes.

It is also essential that you establish with your child that he has 'golden rules', which cannot be countered except by certain people. 'Do Not Leave The School Premises' is one rule that, however much it may *seem* that another adult is telling him to go into town to find Mr M at the swimming pool, cannot be countermanded except on direct instruction by you. Precautions like this may seem overprotective, but it is best to try to anticipate problems before they arise. The consequences of getting it wrong are too serious to risk.

3.9 Request social skills groups

It may be possible to persuade the school to run social skills groups. These are traditionally organized by specialist speech and language therapists, and they might be the best people to approach about setting up a group. A speech and language therapist may be delighted to have the opportunity to come into school, and thereby work with several children 'on her books' at the same time. Even if not available to come into school to run sessions herself, she might be willing to do a training session for staff, or at very least to recommend some good resources and materials to use with the pupils.

The idea of a social skills group is to work with a group of children at all the so-called 'soft skills' – playing together, making and keeping friends, meeting and greeting each other politely, taking turns, resolving disagreements and so on. It is also likely to look at pupils' perceptions of themselves and others, and to do some work on building self-esteem. A social skills group will ideally include a number of children who need help in this area, together with some pupils with highly developed social interaction skills. These children, who are usually highly regarded by their peers and have high social status, will provide good role models for the others, and are often sufficiently confident in themselves to be happy to take less socially adept pupils 'under their wing'. Of course, no one in the group need be aware of why they are there, whether because of social deficit or social strength. The group may be called a 'Focus group to look at friendships', or a 'Sub-committee with responsibility to decide break-time rules', or whatever term seems most appropriate. It can be as simple as a group which meets at lunchtime to play board games (the reason given being that the school wants to try out some games to decide which to buy), and which has a nominated pupil from each year group. In this way the social mix is orchestrated by the teacher, and she or a TA remain on hand to help and guide. The pupils interact. They play the games, take turns, follow the instructions, learn to win and lose – and the adult is there to guide, identify and reinforce positive social behaviour, and to suggest alternatives when behaviour is less successful. When difficulties arise, the teacher or TA has resources to help target that issue, and the group has the time to work at them. Social skills groups are a great use of your TA's allocated time, if you have any, and may be of benefit to many children, not just those with an AS diagnosis.

3.10 Have a whole-staff philosophy (including non-teaching staff)

Sometimes you will be lucky enough to find that the teaching staff at a school, the teachers and TAs, have a good grasp of AS. Perhaps the school instigated introductory training sessions by outside professionals when they became aware that a child in their school had this diagnosis. Perhaps members of staff have been on training sessions, and the school has systems in place to ensure that this training is 'cascaded' down to other members of staff. In this way, what was learnt by one became known by all.

Unfortunately, the people who are left out of this most frequently are just the people who may most need to know. Pupils with AS may be most vulnerable at break- and lunch-times, during swimming lessons taken by outside staff, on the school bus or in after-school clubs. It is the adults who deal with them during these times who are least likely to be given support or training, but who, arguably, may be in most urgent need of that support.

What is needed is a truly whole-school policy on AS. A conscious effort should be made when AS training or awareness is discussed to include lunchtime supervisors, the caretaker, cleaners, the school secretary, parent volunteers, outside sports coaches, drivers and after-school supervisors. It is a sad fact that little of the budget may be available, traditionally, for training these people, but if the pupil with AS is to have his needs met throughout the school day (and not just in the classroom), it is essential that an understanding of AS, and therefore of the pupil's needs, is fostered in all the adults with whom he comes into contact. This may be difficult to achieve, but the school should be encouraged to rise to the challenge. Really meeting the child's needs is not going to happen if there are 'black holes' in the school day when they are not understood.

After-school care may need to be addressed additionally or separately. An after-school club may be run by an organization that is linked to the school in only the loosest of ways. It may be an outside franchise operated by people who have no contact with the school other than using the premises. You will need to discuss your child's needs, and how they are going to be met, with the authorities of this group. Do not assume that just because your child's needs are understood in school that this will automatically continue after school or at breakfast or holiday club activities.

3.11 Look at representation of pupils with AS

Most schools in the twenty-first century are fairly democratic institutions. Most have an elected board or other groups such as parent–teacher associations which have an elected committee. An increasing number of schools also have some sort of school council, a group of pupils elected by their peers whose job it is to make the pupils' views and wishes known to the school authorities.

However, it might be worth investigating to what extent your child's school is working to represent the views of pupils with AS. Is there any policy in place that allows the different needs of pupils with AS to be addressed? It is not enough that they are not excluded from democratic discussion; it may be necessary to take steps to actively include them.

The law in most places requires more than that people with a 'disability' (and for this purpose, AS may be seen as such) are not harassed or discriminated against. Increasingly, schools are required to take a proactive approach, actively promoting equality and positive attitudes in all members of staff and pupils. They need to take into account the effects of AS on a pupil, and to make adjustments for these, even if this means treating the pupil with AS more favourably than his peers because of his AS. They need also to encourage participation of pupils with AS in the life of the school, and to facilitate their preferred ways of communication in order to elicit their views.

It may be that no pupil with AS is elected to the school council via a one-representative-per-class forum. This may not be as a result of discrimination against him, but may be, simply, because a pupil with AS sees the world sufficiently differently that his peers do not consider that he will be best able to represent the mainstream view. They may be right! However, are there steps taken to ensure that the pupil who is elected is able to represent the viewpoint and concerns of all pupils, including those with AS? How often is this, actively, addressed?

It may be that you have to discuss this lack of representation with your child's headteacher, and together come up with a way of making sure that there is no injustice here. One solution may be to appoint a special needs representative on the council, someone (either with or without special needs himself) who makes it his business to find out the views and wishes of all pupils with special needs at the school. How he does this will need consideration. It may be that open group discussions are not the best ways to find out the views of someone with AS. A questionnaire or an online forum may be a more effective tool. It may be necessary to work with pupils with AS in order to find out from them how they would like their views investigated. It is important that this concept is well handled, right from this young age. If the pupil with AS gets used to not being asked his opinion and other pupils get used to not considering his views this may have serious consequences for how the views of adults with AS are heard in later life. You are not being pedantic to insist on this, on everything from group decisions within the classroom about how to manage work, through to the class vote on what game to play. If everyone's view is to be counted, then everyone's view must be sought, even if seeking it takes a little more work — or a different approach — than usual.

3.12 Ask the school to provide a forum to put parents in touch with one another

As discussed earlier (*see* Chapter 1), it may be a great help if you can get together with other parents of children with AS in the school or in the area. This is not primarily because your children will be so alike (they probably won't be much alike at all!), but because many of the issues around AS will be shared. It helps if making this contact may be done with the authority of the school, not least because then the parents will have greater access *to* the school. You may, as a group, decide on ways of raising the AS profile or under-standing, or both, in school, and if you have an element of official sanction, you are better placed to persuade the school to put your ideas into action. If, as a group of parents, you decide that you are a powerful force to help the school (as opposed to criticizing it), you may be able to solve many of the practical problems yourselves. You may form the team that paints the outside play area zones, or that lobbies local businesses to come up with a grant to convert a quiet space. You may access Asperger groups and persuade a speaker to come in to give a training session — to you as parents, and also to staff, both teaching and non-teaching. You may decide between you to form a pool of people with specialist understanding of AS, who may be asked to go along as parent helpers on trips, or who can help each other out by sitting with each other's children when you decide that exams for the child with AS are better done in a room on his own.

There is a real (if subtle) difference if this support group is initiated by the school, rather than being started independently by parents. For a start, it looks less like a protest group, which it may all too easily become if put together by parents who are having trouble with their child's education. If the school has proposed the group, it feels much more like the school is taking the issues seriously and looking for solutions, rather than the parents getting angry and demanding change. It can also feel more formal – perhaps meeting in school, rather than at someone's house. Most importantly, it has a format that welcomes input by teachers, the headteacher and TAs because it is 'their patch', so it is a forum for getting school staff and parents to work together and to share solutions.

As an 'official' school group it goes a long way to overcome the issues raised earlier, about lack of AS representation. It also becomes a way of bridging the home–school divide. It may not work as well as inviting your child's class teacher round for a meal, but it is nevertheless a start at breaking down barriers. It should allow both groups, staff and parents, to better understand the others' point of view. It also 'depersonalizes' issues, in that it moves you away from being one parent expressing concern about some aspect of a teacher's work, and brings you towards being a group of people concerned specifically about the effect of your children's AS on their experience of school.

From the school's point of view, the resourcefulness of starting a discussion group specifically for parents of pupils with AS should be well recognized. It shows that the school is listening and taking AS issues seriously. It is good practice, and should stand the school in excellent stead should their provision for inclusion for pupils with AS ever come under question.

3.13 Educate or inform peers and peers' parents

A school may baulk at all the extra work you are suggesting because pupils with AS in the school are a minority. This is actually irrelevant, since being in a minority does not mean that your needs should not be met. However, in practical terms, it is understandable, if not excusable, that the school may struggle to grasp that it needs to make so many changes to meet the needs of so few pupils.

If you find this, you could point out to the school that the requirement to meet the needs of a pupil with AS is a wider responsibility than to that pupil alone. I have two children, one with AS and one without. I have seen the distress and damage to the education and happiness of my child without AS when she had a child with AS in her class (not mine) *whose needs were not being met*. In this case, it was hard as a parent of a neurotypical child to hear that day after day my daughter's class had to go to the hall because one pupil had barricaded himself under the desk or was threatening his teacher with a chair.

I believe, firmly, that having AS is not a bad thing. I believe also that the needs of a child with AS must be met. If they are not met, it is only too easy (albeit ill-informed) for other parents to see the AS as the problem, rather than the failings of the provision for that child. Unfortunately, there is ignorance and even prejudice among some wider communities. Our children with AS are diplomats for the next generation. One child with AS whose needs are being met and who has no need therefore to be disruptive or aggressive can teach all the others that AS is not a bad thing. One child whose needs are not being met, unfortunately, may do the opposite.

It is essential, of course, that all the adults who care for a child with AS have sufficient training and understanding to be able to do so appropriately. That has to be the first priority. However, there needs to be education of the other children in the class and school as well. How AS is explained or presented to the children, and to the wider community of their parents, will have something to do with this. The school needs to consider and take an active role in deciding how to handle anxiety, concerns and indeed ignorance from other children and parents. You will need to work with the school, and with your child, to decide how to handle this. It takes a great deal of courage and thought to deal with this face-on.

Of course, if other parents are complaining because of your child's disruptive behaviour, it is going to take a rare and brave school indeed to admit that your child behaved in this way not because he has AS but because the school was not meeting the needs of his AS. There are some rare and brave schools out there. It may take courage to see if your child's school is one of them.

3.14 Consider siblings

It may be possible to persuade the school to take the plight of siblings of pupils with AS seriously. These pupils, who do not have AS themselves, nevertheless have to deal with AS in their families every day. They will have to accept that much of their parents' time may be spent on the child with AS, certainly much of their conversation, attention and mental energy. They may have to endure the embarrassment of their sibling calling out in assembly, acting inappropriately at lunchtime, creating a scene during the school play, lying down in the corridor or spinning in the yard. They may feel that they have to prove to pupils and staff alike that they themselves are neurologically 'normal' and that their social skills are developed and mature. They may paradoxically both resent the embarrassment their sibling with AS causes them, and the attention and special treatment which he receives, and at the same time feel highly protective, feeling that they have to explain his behaviour to prevent him getting into trouble, or intervene if he runs into difficulties. I have known parents who had to take their child with

AS out of a school because they were concerned that his sister, at age seven, was having to explain the condition of AS to uncomprehending staff. The strain on a child in this situation is considerable – and it is not her job. The failings of a school regarding its management of pupils with AS must not, at all costs, fall to the child's siblings.

As with so much, awareness of this is the best start. If the sibling is older, there is the advantage that he or she moves through the school first and so has a chance to establish him or herself. If younger, it is imperative that comparisons are not made, even (or perhaps especially) favourable ones. School staff will need also to be sensitive to how long the diagnosis of AS has been in place. A family may well be still reeling with shock if the diagnosis has been recent. Having to redraw your family as one that has a member with AS can be a shock, and the sibling of the child with the diagnosis may be suffering considerable anxiety and strain. Perhaps he or she has many questions to ask yet no one has yet had the time to address them. If his or her teacher has good understanding of AS, she may well be an excellent person for the sibling to turn to, and this may feel natural to the child. It is important that the teacher has sufficient understanding to be able to answer these questions and insecurities with well-informed knowledge.

You may need to make a request to your children's school formally that your neurotypical child or children be 'protected' from the effects of having a sibling with AS at the same establishment. You may together decide a policy that the children are never put to work in the same team, for example on sports day. You may have to make sure that break-time supervisors are sensitive to protecting your neurotypical child from involvement in disputes involving your child with AS. On the other hand, your neurotypical child may feel genuinely protective, and want to take an active role in including their sibling with AS in school activities, and raising the profile and understanding of AS. It may be that the sibling of a child with AS is the ideal choice for the position of special needs representative on the school council. Just as with the child with AS, the management of the situation needs to start with the individuals themselves. Making the school aware of the issue should be enough: it should be well-placed to manage the situation from there on.

3.15 Review sex education policy

By the end of the age range covered in this book (four- to ten-year-olds), many schools will have begun to implement a sex education policy. However difficult you may find it to talk about this issue, it will be necessary to be very proactive about discussing this policy with the school. Indeed, doing so is good practice for you, as it is an issue that is going to become even more important over the next few years. It is probably best to bite the bullet and to get used to making appointments to discuss sex with the headteacher now! After all, with practice it may get easier.

This is, in fact, a serious issue. How sexual matters, body changes, physical urges and responses are explained to the child with AS can have a profound effect on his future happiness. If you pretend the situation does not exist you will not be in a position to guide him through this minefield. Your child is going to need explicit teaching about 'appropriate and inappropriate' behaviour, and you are going to have to put in a great deal of work to ensure that the messages that you give him are consistent with the messages he is given at school. At very least, this means making yourself familiar with what is taught at school.

The most likely subjects to be covered with this age range are concerned with personal hygiene and body changes. Find out what the school line on these is going to be. If you cannot agree with it, you will need to remove your child from the lessons. What he does not need, as a young person with AS, is ambiguity. If the school says that it is necessary for young people to take a shower every day, you are going to have to make sure that the bathroom is made available to him every day (and that you have a shower attachment fitted). If the school suggests the use of underarm deodorant, you will need to buy some for him. If the school nurse, or whichever teacher is taking the session, says that sweat smells disgusting, you may have to cope with self-loathing or at very least, frequent clothes-changing in your child. These are powerful messages about a subject that worries most young people. You would do well to prepare your child before the official lessons start.

This is perhaps even more important when the subject under discussion is the changes of puberty. I suggest that you familiarize your child with AS with the facts about these changes long before they are brought up in school. Make sure that he has a good, scientifically accurate grasp of what the changes of puberty are going to bring to his body – and to the bodies of the others around him – and a likely timescale for these changes. For many people with AS change brings anxiety, and puberty is change at a fundamental level. He is going to need consistent, calm, repeated, fact-based information to help him deal with this subject. As a parent you are going to have to take responsibility for this, and not leave it to the school. Find out from the school when these subjects are discussed, and make sure you get in there well ahead of them. You will need also to ensure that your son has a confident grasp of facts before the schoolyard rumours on the subject start to circulate. He is going to be very vulnerable to the misinformation and jokes which abound at this time.

3.16 Consider teacher personality

Much is written, both here in this book and elsewhere, about the importance of AS awareness and training. It is, of course, important. However, it is not the be-all and end-all. The very best teacher my child ever had, had no AS training whatsoever and had never taught a child with AS before. What she was, was a naturally gifted teacher, a wonderful communicator, someone who loved her job and was full of enthusiasm every day. She never saw our child's AS as a problem. Indeed, she enjoyed it and welcomed it, and he very quickly learnt to do so, too. She liked him, AS and all, and he thrived under her care.

Some teachers will work better with your child than others. As a broad rule, it seems to be teachers who lack confidence themselves who are most likely to worry the child with AS. If the teacher gets cross or shouts, your child may not realize that the teacher is not shouting at him and may well still become distressed. If the teacher says that there will be three parts to the lesson, and then through poor time management only has time for two, this is likely again to unsettle the pupil with AS. It is hard to quantify what makes a 'good teacher', but children know. It is, unfortunately, a fact that some teachers do struggle some of the time.

If your child with AS begins to struggle at school where previously he was managing well it may be down to the personality or skill of his current teacher. This can be a tricky matter to address. On the whole, the best solution is likely to be to discuss the issue, in non-emotive terms, with the headteacher. A good headteacher will face up to the issue and will know what to do in a way that supports all parties. This is an area where you are going to have to trust your headteacher's professional judgement and to trust both her willingness and her ability to act.

3.17 Facilitate school-wide communication

The most common theme of this book is probably the need for communication. As parents, you need open and frequent communication with the adults who work with your child – the teacher or TA. You need also to have a good line of communication with the headteacher to discuss matters of policy and to work together on an overview of your child's care. You need to facilitate communication between the various specialists who may be working with your child and with the school, and between the current research in the field of AS and the adults 'on the ground'. You need to find ways of helping your child with AS to communicate. You may support him through the use of laptop, or diary, or through visual supports such as 'angry cards'. You need to help his TA and his teacher to communicate with him, supporting the use of non-figurative language, and to help him communicate with his peers and they with him. You may help the school to improve its use of communication around the building, whether it be through the use of labelling and directions, or through the open disclosure of school rules or timetables for the day or week. You may try to facilitate communication within the school, between teachers who have worked with your child before, between TAs and teachers, and between teaching and non-teaching staff. You may hope that there can be open communication between you and the other parents at the school, both with those whose child shares a similar diagnosis and with those whose children do not.

It is worth discussing lines of communication with the headteacher as a matter of school policy. You may be able to devise solutions. Perhaps something as simple as a notice board outside the school each morning, which lists which members of staff are away and who will stand in for them, could make a difference. Perhaps there could be an update on the website each morning which lists changes to the usual routine. Of all the school policies, good communication is likely to be the most important to you as a parent of a pupil with AS, and it needs to be truly school-wide, not merely left to individuals. As with so much to do with AS, what makes good practice for the child with AS is usually of benefit to other pupils as well. Good communication is seldom a bad thing!

4

Quick Reference: What to Do when Things go Wrong

Philosophy and long-term planning are all very well, but what do you do in a crisis?

One of the most frightening aspects of observing pupils with AS in school, as I said in Chapter 3, is just how quickly things may go wrong. It is important to have a strategy in place so that damage may be minimized and everyone can get back on track as quickly as possible. This section looks at the 'quick fix' solutions: the ways you, as a parent, can intervene immediately to try to prevent further damage.

Flare-ups, 'aggression' and running away are all examples of the child in crisis. To feel the need to shout, hit, kick or escape, the pupil is likely to be pretty desperate. It is essential to explore the desperation, not merely react to the child's behaviour.

4.1 Provide 'space'

The first response to behaviour of this kind should be to give the pupil with AS space. Ideally, in school this space will have been formalized, as a 'quiet space' somewhere in the school or at least in the classroom. The child should be able to access this space before being overwhelmed, so that it provides prevention rather than cure. If problems are occurring it may be that the pupil is not able to access his space, perhaps because he or the adults involved do not fully understand the process. A card that the child can present when he needs space is more effective than his having to ask for it, as communication skills are likely to be the first to fail when the pupil with AS is feeling overwhelmed. The fact that there has been a flare-up indicates that this system is not working in your child's case. As a parent, you are in the strongest position to grant your child space: *keep him home from school until the problem has been resolved.* This may be hugely inconvenient, but until the reasons for your son's flare-up have been understood and addressed the problem still exists and is only going to escalate. If your son has had to shout, bite, kick or run away, there is a serious issue and he is communicating this as strongly as he is able. As his parent, you need to listen.

4.2 Do not punish the behaviour

Part of the problem of finding out that your child has behaved in these ways is that it feels that it reflects on you. Biting, kicking and hitting can look like the result of bad parenting, and, more importantly, they *feel* like the result of bad parenting. It is very hard not to be furious with your child for 'letting me down', and to focus only on the behaviour: 'How *dare* you bite the teacher! I am ashamed of you, and I am going to punish you by taking away all your computer games and you needn't think you're going swimming tonight either…'

Imagine you are standing on a train platform. Someone comes up to you and tells you to jump on the tracks. Of course you refuse, since you know it is 'wrong'. When the person repeats his demand you turn your back and walk away. At this point, the person grabs your arm and drags you towards the platform edge. You are terrified. You know that an express train is due through the station in seconds. You struggle. You yell, you kick, you bite. When you break free you run off the station as fast as you can.

When we punish our children with AS for their 'unacceptable behaviour', we may be missing the point. In the example above, any one of us 'neurotypical' adults would bite and shout, and we would not feel any need to apologize for this behaviour. We would feel that the situation clearly warranted it. How unjust it would feel to us if, when the police arrived, we were arrested and punished for our behaviour.

The point is: *extreme behaviour is understandable if a person feels himself under extreme threat.* When responding to this sort of behaviour in our children with AS, it is essential always to understand what prompted the behaviour.

4.3 Treat the cause, not the effect, and provide an alternative response

It may take some detective work to find out what really went wrong. If the school has been keeping a pupil incident log, reading this may help you and the school to understand the trigger for your child's behaviour. Your child is the best person to explain it, but he will need to be given the chance to calm down and 'regroup' first. He may need considerable prompting (being taken back to the place where the incident happened, going through events 'frame by frame') and support to be able to articulate it. It is well worth spending time doing this. If the child is able to articulate the trigger, often it may be examined, changed, explained or removed. More importantly for your child's long-term welfare, he can be helped to explore alternative reactions. If our adult on the train platform had had a personal alarm, she could have triggered that as an alternative to fighting back, and it may well have been as effective. *We need to arm our children with AS with alternate strategies that work* before we even begin to reprimand them for using the only strategies which they currently have available.

4.4 Don't reinforce the wrong behaviour

Kyle, a five-year-old pupil with AS, had his peg in the middle of the cloakroom. He started the school year well. The weather was sunny, and at the beginning of break-time the children went straight outside to play. As autumn set in, Kyle started to spit at his fellow pupils. He spat frequently in the cloakroom and even began doing so in class. Kyle was reprimanded for his spitting and even punished, but it made no difference.

The origin of Kyle's spitting was traced back. As the weather had become colder, the cloakroom had become extremely crowded before each break-time as children scrabbled for coats. One day, mimicking his family cat, Kyle hissed and spat at the boy next to him who was jostling him. He was seen by the teacher, who 'punished' him by sending him back into the classroom (which was quiet and empty), and told him to wait until last to collect his coat and go out to play.

From that time on, Kyle used spitting. Although it did not always work, it worked so often that when Kyle felt threatened because people were too close to him, spitting either made them move away from him or allowed him to be removed to a 'quiet space'. Kyle's behaviour was a direct result of the actions of the teacher who had reinforced precisely the behaviour she sought to eliminate.

The solution to Kyle's spitting was to respect his need to wait in the classroom until the cloakroom was clearer before fetching his coat. He was also given an alternative strategy to spitting which worked just as well (in Kyle's case a phrase, 'Please will you step back' that he could use in the classroom to indicate that he needed more space).

When dealing with 'unacceptable behaviour' in a child with AS, *it is important that we are aware that our reaction to it may become a reinforcer.* Incidentally, this might be a problem with the advice given earlier. If lashing out results in a day or two off school, this may itself reinforce the action. Nothing is ever simple! On the other hand, if your child is that keen to get out of school by any means, perhaps this is indicative of a bigger problem.

4.5 Be your child's 'AS interpreter'

In the incident of the broken window, mentioned in Chapter 3, it became obvious that interpretation of what happened was the key. It is essential when dealing with an incident to *understand what happened from the point of view of the person with AS.* One of the least effective responses is to jump to conclusions. However well-meaning, neither anger management support nor help joining in the game of football would have made any sense to the child who put his fist through the window. Before we even begin to deal with an incident, we need to know what it is that has gone wrong. As parents, we have the most time, the best understanding of our child and, to be honest, the greatest motivation to find out what really happened. When things go wrong at school, become involved straightaway. Support the school staff, but make sure that your child's AS is not discounted. Some schools have policies such as 'Zero tolerance of bad behaviour'. You can support this policy – indeed, you can demand just these high expectations of your child. However, you need to be there to ensure that what he did was, actually, bad behaviour. If what he did made sense to him, was what he believed was expected or required, or was as a result of fear or the belief that he was in danger, this is not 'bad behaviour'.

4.6 Locate the trigger

When your child behaves 'badly' there will be a reason for it. Too often the focus is on *what* the child with AS has done, and not enough on *why* he did it. Sometimes, as in the examples above, the two may be linked, but often they will not be.

The first thing to check is your child himself. If he is in pain, this may manifest itself in 'bad' behaviour. Ask him very specific, calm questions about if he has a pain in his ear/head/tummy, and if necessary take him to the doctor to have him checked out. Less dramatically, wait a day and see if a cold or a stomach upset develops. Very often apparently unco-operative or defiant behaviour will have its roots internally, and many an incident of 'aggression' in a child with AS has been traced to an ear infection.

If the child is physically well, the next thing for you to check is his emotional well-being. He may have misunderstood something and be suffering anxiety or even fear. There is a story, which may be apocryphal, but tells of a boy with AS who refused to go into town after he heard his father give directions and refer to the 'Green Dragon'. No one had told the boy that this was the name of a restaurant, and he was terrified. Sadly, the condition of having AS can bring with it huge levels of anxiety, and you will need to work with your child to find out exactly what it is that is worrying him.

Finally, *you would do well to ask yourself, 'What has changed?'* Very often an incident of 'misbehaviour' will be linked to change. Ben, aged six, was being observed in school and was managing very well. He was calm, co-operative and focussed on a task. However, when he came in from break-time he upturned all the trays of pencils, spilling them all on the floor and throwing the empty trays at the wall. He was taken to the study where he hid inside a large cardboard box. It turned out that usually, on a Tuesday, a different teacher took the session after play-time, but that this Tuesday Ben's usual teacher had stayed on, precisely because Ben was being observed. She had believed that this would give a fairer, more consistent environment for Ben – but had not told him of the change. The incident could have been avoided if Ben had been prepared for the change in routine, and could have been contained if he had been given the tools to request access to a safe 'quiet space' in a more appropriate way. Neither the lack of preparation nor the lack of appropriate tools was Ben's fault, so it would have been unfair in this incidence if he had found himself in trouble.

What has commonly changed when things go wrong at school is the underlying structure. One of the worst times for a pupil with AS is the end of term. The routines of school, which he has probably learned to rely on, begin to fall apart. School trips are organized, 'fun' days appear, sports days are timetabled, then rained off, then re-timetabled. Perhaps there are also end-of-term parties, school plays, non-uniform or fancy dress days. New teachers visit and current teachers are absent as they visit their new schools. There is talk about some pupils leaving the school and moving on, and about all pupils having to move classrooms or teachers, having to move or change lockers and pack up their possessions. Is it surprising that with so many changes, the child with AS becomes distressed? It may feel as if your child can no longer manage the school environment, but it may only be that he cannot manage the environment for the final week of term. There is much to be said for taking him out for the last week, and booking an early holiday. You will avoid all sorts of stress – and the holiday may well be cheaper as well!

4.7 Check level of understanding

Your child may or may not have an above-average intelligence quotient (IQ). He may or may not talk like a 'Little Professor'. What he may very likely be experiencing, though, is lack of understanding. It is not uncommon for the verbosity and extensive vocabulary of a child with AS to mask lack of comprehension. Just because he can list the plant-life of the Cretaceous Period does not mean that he understood that he was supposed to come in from the playground when the whistle was blown. It is far more likely that your child is experiencing confusion in school, rather than being defiant.

If your child seems to be doing something 'wrong', you need to *check that he understands what is needed to do it 'right'*. Many acts of apparent non-compliance, rudeness or aggression may be traced to lack of social understanding. Work with the school on addressing the confusion before either it or you begin to contemplate what to do about 'naughtiness'.

4.8 Check that you are clear about what you want

It may be that the crisis is not in your child at all. It is in you. You begin to feel that things are not going well, that your child is not joining in, that he is not getting as much out of school as you would hope. Perhaps he is not achieving as well as you had hoped academically. Perhaps he seems isolated and lonely. You begin to feel restless and that the school is not doing all it should to support him.

This low-level dissatisfaction may grow and grow until you storm into a parents' consultation meeting with all verbal guns blazing. Few things could be more destructive.

To identify the problems, you need to ask yourself if you and the school are really 'pulling in the same direction'. *Do you know what you want from the experience of sending your child to school?* Does the school want the same things? What does your child want? What criteria are going to be used to measure success? What does the school want from you as parents? What does it expect from your child? Are the school's criteria the same as yours, or different?

These questions, although seldom asked, lie at the heart of a successful relationship between parents and school. If these questions are not asked, and the philosophy behind them is not agreed and clarified by both parties, it may be that parents and school are working to different ends. What is seen as a success by one party may be seen as a failure by the other. It is hardly surprising if the child with AS becomes lost and confused in the middle of all this.

The parents of a child with AS may have very different expectations from education than the parents of a neurotypical child, and one parent of a child with AS may well differ in his wishes from another. One parent might want raised self-esteem whilst another really wants compliance. A third may be concerned only with academic progress. Similarly, a teacher may view success in terms of what is achieved academically, in terms of what is learnt (which may be different), or in terms of the behaviour of the pupil. She may feel that there is pressure on her to make a child with AS conform to certain behavioural rules because of the underlying expectations placed upon her by the school. She may feel that her credibility as a teacher would be undermined if a pupil in her class failed to sit quietly with the other pupils when asked to do so, or read a book while the other pupils were involved in a group activity. She may feel that it reflects badly on her if a pupil in her class sits under the table for the whole of the science lesson – even though that child's science attainment may be considerably above average. Conversely, in this increasingly performance-driven world, both school and individual teacher may feel pressure to achieve certain results with a child with AS. Perhaps his high IQ score preceded him to school, and the staff fear that if his attainment does not match his potential, they will be held accountable.

What is needed is for school and parents to sit down together and work out a clear description of what they each want for the child. What do they think will qualify as 'success' for that child in that school, and how are they going to measure this success?

As a parent you need to be very clear about your long-term objectives. You need to be clear in your own mind what you want the process of 'going to school' to achieve for your child. Perhaps one way to do this is to turn the question around and to ask yourself, 'What do I want for my child as an adult?' When you are clear on that, you can be clearer about what he needs to learn or gain between then and now, and how best to go about helping him to do that.

This is a bigger issue than you might realize. Perhaps, in your heart of hearts, what you want for your child as an adult is for him not to have AS any more. It is a small step from that to realizing that what you want from school is that it 'cures' him. You want school somehow to make your child 'the same as everyone else', to make him behave like the other pupils, have friends, be picked for the school teams, do well in tests, be articulate, literate and numerate, and generally to be a social and academic success. Is it surprising, if this is your hidden agenda – hidden perhaps even from yourself – that the school is going to fail to deliver?

Understanding this is a huge first step. However, the next step is important, too: you need to communicate to the school that you are not expecting it to deliver a 'cure'. Much of the stress and pressure on the teachers of a child with AS come from feeling that they must make the child behave like the other pupils and achieve like his peers. Articulating that you are not expecting this; indeed, that you do not want this, may make a great difference to how the school faces the challenge of educating your child with AS.

None of this is to say that your expectations for your child with AS are in any way lowered. Rather the reverse. You do not want a 'cure' because there is nothing wrong with your child! What you want is that his AS is accepted. You want it to be accommodated and that his needs because of it are included in the philosophy of the school. That is what 'inclusion' in education means.

4.9 Consider giving up…

It may seem rather sad to end this book on ways to support your child with AS in school with the advice to consider giving up. On the other hand, the knowledge that there is a 'get-out clause' may be the very thing that takes the pressure off. Most countries, states and districts require in law that children be educated full-time. They do not require that this happens in school. Eventually, if having followed all the advice in this book, having been involved, worked with the staff, joined with other parents and communicated tirelessly, your child with AS remains unhappy in a school environment, you may always consider taking him out. Your child need not go to school.

Your child need not go to school! Your child need not go to *that* particular school (you could find another), and indeed your child need not go to *any* school. This concept may be like a flash of light to some parents, and to some children with AS.

Home-educating your child may sound like a huge and drastic step (particularly if you have not considered it before). In fact, it is not such an amazing idea. Parents the world over do teach their own children. Home-education groups exist in most places. There is probably one very close to where you live. Once you take it on board, it is not such an outrageous idea after all.

The point, as relevant to this book, on how to make school make sense for your child with AS, is: *school is not the only option*. If your child need not go to school, then it follows that you choose that he goes there. He is at school by choice. This simple fact may, in itself, be enough to solve 90 per cent of the problems you and your child are experiencing. It is one thing to be struggling desperately to try to improve a compulsory inappropriate environment. It is something else entirely to choose to 'try out' an environment, to see if it may be made to work for your child and, if not, to walk away. If you and your child know that school is not the only option, how much more likely is it that you can work with its idiosyncrasies, tolerate some of its inconsistencies, be amused together by its inappropriateness? Knowing that it is not compulsory takes much of the heat out of the 'problem' that is school, and allows a far more relaxed, positive attitude to making it work.

It can work. School can 'make sense' to the child with AS. Yes, it is a challenging and often confusing environment; there are, of course, many problems which a child with AS may encounter at school. However, there is also much that may be done to help, and most of it is infinitely 'do-able'. The practical, accessible suggestions given in this book are a great place to start.

As the parent of a child with AS, you are the key. You have the motivation to be the 'bridge' that links home and school. You are the 'other-half' of your child's education providing the social, sensory, cognitive and communicative solutions to the many challenges that he faces. You are also the person who loves him for who he is. It is easy as 'outsiders' to see AS only as a problem or a challenge. That is only half the picture.

The following excerpt was written by Sam, a boy of seven who has AS. What is clear from Sam's description is that he does not see the world of school as an impossible, or even a hostile place. His struggle seems to be that, although there is much about it he finds attractive, it just is not as engaging as the world in his head.

I have Asperger syndrome.

Having AS means that I am clever and I have a different brain. But I don't find everything easier – oh no! With me, my mind always dreams off into another world when I'm supposed to be writing, and sometimes I can't help reading (but that's probably because I'm almost totally consumed by that!). And sometimes I find it quite hard to 'go with the flow', as in do what everyone else is doing. When that happens, I once again begin to dream off into another world.

When I am at school I have to prevent this from happening. (It does happen in school sometimes still!) I have to try not to allow the real world to be pushed away, like with a force field, by my other world. If it does, I find it hard to notice things that my teacher, or somebody else, says. Sometimes teachers talking to me have to say things twice (or more!) to get my attention. And sometimes I get distracted and start reading when someone is talking to me. You might think that I'm being silly or unfriendly even, but really I'm taken up by it and don't mean to be unfriendly at all. I do want to be friendly – I love making friends – but my total body-want to read or go into a dream sometimes takes over my brain.

When I get home I can go off into my other world and let out all my stress and all that. My other world is my world. It is extremely important to me, and is very real to me (although I know it is not real for anyone else.)

I like my brain being able to go off, but I don't want it to happen too often. More importantly, I want to be in charge of when I go off. I want to be able to play, make friends, join in the real world, but still – when I want to – go into my world...and then back into the real world. My world to me is a wonderful place. It is like having a laptop computer in my head that always has an internet connection to my memory. I can describe what it is like to go off into my world when I want to – it is BRILLIANT! But the real world is brilliant too.

School can be made to 'Make Sense' for the child with AS. He can enjoy school, his AS accommodated and allowed for, and he can find school a huge help in learning to live happily with having AS. What we must do, though, is to make sure that we respect the 'different-ness' of the child with AS, and accept his needs and wants. After all, wouldn't most of us, if we had access to an 'internet connection to our memories', choose to log into it at various points in the day?

AS is something to work with, not something to defeat. If all the parties involved – school staff, parents and pupils – work together, respect each other, make allowances for one anothers' differences, and, above all, keep communicating, there can be a bright future for us all. Good luck!

Index

Create a Reward Plan for your Child with Asperger Syndrome
John Smith, Jane Donlan and Bob Smith
Paperback, ISBN: 978-1-84310-622-7, 112pp

Reward plans encourage positive behaviour using the incentive of earning rewards. This book provides a thorough nuts-and-bolts guide to creating a reward plan for your child with Asperger Syndrome (AS) to help him or her develop positive behaviours, such as social and communication skills.

John Smith, Jane Donlan and their son Bob, who was diagnosed with AS at age eight, explain the importance of keeping a reward plan positive, specific and challenging enough to be stimulating. Helping your child to learn about positive behaviour while gaining a sense of achievement, a reward plan increases self-esteem, confidence and independence.

Create a Reward Plan for your Child with Asperger Syndrome is full of advice and practical suggestions for how to tailor a reward plan to meet your child's specific needs.

Playing, Laughing and Learning with Children on the Autism Spectrum
A Practical Resource of Play Ideas for Parents and Carers
Second Edition
Julia Moor
Paperback, ISBN: 978-1-84310-060-7, 304pp

'An approachable and practical edition that will
be welcomed by parents and carers alike. I know
how hard it can be to find "How to" resources for parents. Well here
is a gem.'

– Children, Young People and Families

Parents of young children newly diagnosed as on the autism
spectrum are often at a loss for ideas about how best to help their
child. *Playing, Laughing and Learning with Children on the Autism
Spectrum* is not just a collection of play ideas; it shows how to break
down activities into manageable stages, and looks at ways to gain a
child's attention and motivation and to build on small achievements.

Each chapter covers a collection of ideas around a theme,
including music, art, physical activities, playing outdoors, puzzles,
turn-taking and using existing toys to create play sequences. There
are also chapters on introducing reading and making the most of
television. This updated second edition contains an extensive
chapter on how to use the computer, the internet, and the digital
camera to find and make resources and activities, and suggests
many suitable websites to help parents through the internet maze.
The ideas are useful both for toddlers and primary age children
who are still struggling with play.

Reaching and Teaching the Child with Autism Spectrum Disorder
Using Learning Preferences and Strengths
Heather MacKenzie
Paperback, ISBN: 978-1-84310-623-4, 272pp

Reaching and Teaching the Child with Autism Spectrum Disorder provides a positive approach to understanding and educating children on the autism spectrum. The book gives greater insight intoSpectrum Disorder the perspective and behavior of a child with autism and explores how the child's learning preferences, strengths and interests can be used to facilitate learning and enhance motivation.

Based on well-researched theory and extensive clinical experience, the author provides a comprehensive model for developing lifelong independent learning skills in children with autism between the ages of 3 and 12 years old. The book describes the underlying principles, learning preferences and strengths typical of children with autism and offers a detailed but flexible program structure based on these concepts. Easy-to-follow activities and approaches are described in each chapter, along with clear examples and illustrations.

This accessible and practical book is an essential resource for parents, teachers, support workers, therapists and others concerned with learning and development in children with autism.

A Will of His Own
Reflections on Parenting a Child with Autism
Revised Edition
Kelly Harland
Foreword by Jane Asher
Paperback, ISBN: 978-1-84310-869-6, 160pp

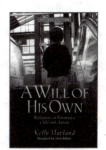

"Kelly Harland's wonderfully clear, unsentimental and yet moving account of her daily struggles with Will brings a whole new perspective to our understanding [of autism]. Her descriptions of the continually changing hopes and aspirations that she and her husband have for him will have echoes for every parent, especially those of children affected by this complex, multi-faceted condition."

—from the Foreword by Jane Asher,
President of The National Autistic Society

Kelly Harland's stories explore her son's life to the age of 14, and the new and unexpected universe she and her husband—both professional musicians—must learn to navigate with him.

Will's fears, anxieties, and obsessions can dominate daily life, making a trip to the grocery store seem like a walk across a minefield. But amidst these unpredictable "flip-outs" and "freak-outs," there are moments of wonder. When Will finally learns the give and take of conversation, or dreams about his future, it rekindles his mother's belief that anything is possible.

Asperger's Syndrome in Young Children
A Developmental Guide for Parents and Professionals
Laurie Leventhal-Belfer and Cassandra Coe
Paperback, ISBN: 978-1-84310-748-4, 304pp

This landmark book focuses on how Asperger's Syndrome (AS) presents in young children. An essential guide for parents coming to terms with their child's AS diagnosis and for the professionals who work with this age group, it is unique in answering pressing questions specific to younger children. How can parents help their AS child to develop speech and language? What help is available at school and home? When, if at all, should a child be informed about AS? Including a useful summary of early childhood development stages, Leventhal-Belfer and Coe provide a diagnostic model based on assessment of the child in contrast to 'neurotypical' children, considering relationships at home, in school or in care. Their book shows how to develop tailored early intervention strategies and to assist parents, teachers and mental health professionals in making informed decisions to nurture the development of AS children.